THE HEAVENS
ARE EMPTY

THE HEAVENS ARE EMPTY

Discovering the Lost Town of Trochenbrod

AVROM BENDAVID-VAL

PEGASUS BOOKS

NEW YORK

THE HEAVEN ARE EMPTY

Pegasus Books LLC
80 Broad Street, 5th Floor
New York, NY 10004

First Pegasus Books cloth edition 2010
First Pegasus Books trade paperback edition 2011

Interior design by Maria Fernandez

ISBN: 978-1-60598-291-5

10 9 8 7 6 5 4 3 2 1

Printed in the United States of America
Distributed by W. W. Norton & Company, Inc.

ON THE WATER

by Yisrael Beider

My brothers have reached the far shore,
Landed on solid ground.
I alone remain, mid way,
My ship heavily burdened.

I was late, thought I could hurry and reach the
    other side.
But then, night fell.
And who knows how long until day.
The ground where I stand is like the froth on the
    water.

I see a little star,
A sparkling from far away.
My brothers are sending greetings to me.
Their flame burns there on the other side.

This poem, originally in Yiddish, was found among newspaper clip-
pings that Yonteleh Beider had saved. It was written by his brother
and probably published around 1939 in Podlaiyisher Tzeitung *(the*
Podlayisher Newspaper), in Mezerich, Poland, where he was living at
the time. The Podlayisher Tzeitung *published many Yiddish poems*
by Yisrael Beider.

This book is dedicated to my father, YomTov (Yonteleh) Beider from Trochenbrod. He went to Palestine in 1932, changed his name to Chagai Bendavid, immigrated to the United States in 1939, and died thirty years later in Washington, D.C. He mentioned Trochenbrod infrequently, yet his longing and affection for it were unmistakable. The memory of that affection impelled me to find a way to stand where that mysterious place was, to try to feel the soul of it, and inspired the years of research that led to this book.

Chagai Bendavid is the one holding the cigarette in this photo of a construction crew in Tel Aviv, in 1934.

CONTENTS

Preface *Next Year in Trochenbrod*
by Jonathan Safran Foer xiii

Introduction *The Back Story* xvii

Chapter One *The First Hundred Years* 1

Chapter Two *Between the Wars* 37

Chapter Three *Dusk* 79

Chapter Four *Darkness* 101

Epilogue *The Story Continues* 141

Witnesses Remember 157

Glossary of Hebrew and Yiddish Terms 191

Chronology 197

Sources 203

Acknowledgments 213

Preface

NEXT YEAR IN
TROCHENBROD

I f the Diaspora could be run backward, if Jewish history, itself, could be funneled and compressed into a single location—some place that captured the vibrancy and catastrophe, the yearning, invention and destruction—we might find ourselves in Trochenbrod. The more I've learned about the singular shtetl—and the great portion of my knowledge comes from the book in your hands—the more strongly I feel that it was the most special place ever to have existed.

In 2002, I contributed my novel, *Everything is Illuminated,* to the small and diverse library of books devoted to Trochenbrod. It is a highly fictionalized response to a trip I made, as a twenty-year-old student, in an effort to find the woman who saved my grandfather, Louis Safran, from the Nazis. The book was an experiential, rather than historical, record of Trochenbrod. Or perhaps it's more accurate to say it was a deeply personal expression of one young man's experience in his destroyed ancestral homeland.

The Heavens are Empty is the definitive history of this definitive place. If this book feels more fantastical than my novel, or than any novel you've ever read, it is because of Trochenbrod's ingenuity, the Holocaust's ferocity, and Bendavid-Val's heroic research and pitch-perfect storytelling. This rigorously journalistic book reads at times like science fiction, at times like magical realism, at times like a thriller, and always like a tragedy. You might find yourself crying most at the parts that aren't sad.

Jews conclude the Passover *seder*—the recounting of the Exodus from Egypt, and perpetually relevant movement toward freedom—with the words, "Next year in Jerusalem." It's an odd statement, as most of us who live outside of Jerusalem could, if we wanted, be in Jerusalem this year. We are not there because we choose not to be.

But the statement does not refer to a Jerusalem that can be found on a map; it refers to an idea. Next year in a place of redemption, a place where the shards of creation are gathered together and we are more like the stories we tell ourselves about ourselves.

Trochenbrod will never be redeemed, and we will never, next year, be there. The dead cannot be brought back to life, the buildings cannot rise from the earth. The Diaspora cannot be run backward. And yet here we are, readers of this book, citizens of that place.

Trochenbrod was the most special place ever to have existed. Not *was* . . . *is*.

—JONATHAN SAFRAN FOER
Brooklyn, New York

Introduction

THE BACK STORY

There once was a town called Trochenbrod in what today is western Ukraine. It had dozens of businesses of all kinds, and people would travel from all around to shop, work, and sell there. Trochenbrod had a post office, a police station, a fire brigade, a cultural center, schools, and everything you'd expect in a small but lively town. It's gone now. A trail for tractors and horse-drawn wagons through empty land is all that remains of the once bustling street that ran through the town.

My father never described his home town (pronounced TRAW-khen-brawd) to me; and I, growing up in 1950s and

'60s America, never thought to ask. Yet every once in a while my father would happen to mention it, and when he did, he said "Trochenbrod" with a tone that conveyed longing, loving remembrance, and sadness, but he also said it with a slight twist of his mouth, a sort of half smile that hinted at "funny little place." After he was gone, all I knew of Trochenbrod was the sense of it that my father had conveyed by his way of saying the name. Relatives told me that Trochenbrod no longer existed, but that had no meaning for me. I had never seen proof that it once existed, any more than I had seen proof that it no longer existed. Trochenbrod was only a vague shadow in my imagination, so how could it no longer exist?

Trochenbrod suddenly stopped being only a shadow in my imagination when for forgotten reasons I found myself in a Mormon family research center, decided to search for Trochenbrod, and discovered my first factual representation of it in print: its coordinates 50°55′21.68″ north, 25°42′07.54″ east. Under the coordinates was an explanation that the town had many Jews; was known by two names, Trochenbrod and Sofiyovka; and was completely destroyed in the Holocaust. Instantly it was real: a place that really once was, and that really is no more. It had two names, so it couldn't have been just a no-place, I supposed. What might still be there? There had to be at least some signs of buildings that once were there, at those coordinates.

Thoughts like these floated occasionally around the edges of my consciousness as I went about my career in economic development in poor countries, until one day working in Warsaw I realized that where Trochenbrod had been situated was just over the border and a bit south in Ukraine. Visiting it should not be too difficult. Why not do it? The year was 1997. I found my way to the phone number of a young man in Lviv who was beginning to build a business of genealogical research for Jewish families and was willing to serve as a guide, translator, and driver for people like me. We talked over the terms and agreed on date for a trip to find Trochenbrod in November of that year.

The young man's name was Alexander Dunai. About ten years later Alex was described with great affection by another customer-become-friend, Daniel Mendelsohn, in his book, *The Lost: A Search for Six of Six Million*. Alex helped Daniel visit a small town in Ukraine where members of his family had lived and were murdered, and to research what happened there, during some of the time when he was also helping me.

To prepare for the trip I visited the Library of Congress. There I found, among other things, a Russian map from the late 1800s, and with the help of the coordinates I was able to locate Trochenbrod on it. The map was delicately drawn. When I photocopied the area around Trochenbrod in larger scale I could see the town's outline and the trails running through it; it was almost like having an aerial photograph of Trochenbrod. I quickly walked outside the august building so I could let go a shout of excitement. Pieces were falling into place. I couldn't wait to get to Ukraine.

When I think back on that day I find myself smiling—not at how excited and eager I was, but rather at my innocence. I didn't have the slightest idea that what I would experience and discover on each visit to Trochenbrod and the surrounding area would make me feel I had to return there to dig deeper, and that this would happen again and again for more than a decade. I didn't have the slightest idea that I was about to fall under the spell of a vanished place, vanished people, a vanished civilization and its rich culture, even vanished nations, and new nations, all intertwined with historic currents and cataclysms. I didn't have the slightest idea that to know Trochenbrod I would have to learn about many aspects of world history I knew nothing about before, so I was about to commit to the biggest research project of my life. I didn't have the slightest idea that I was about to embark on an odyssey more enriching than anything I had ever experienced.

My brother Marvin and I, with a copy of the map in hand, landed in the small and quirky Soviet-era airport for the city of Lviv, beautifully modeled after an old-fashioned railroad station. Known as Lvov in earlier days, Lviv is the de facto capital of western Ukraine. We were met by our jovial and slightly rotund Alex with his faithful Lada—the USSR's version of a 1972 Fiat. We looked around Lviv a bit and then headed off on the ninety-five-mile drive northeast to the city of Lutsk. Ukraine was in its early post-Communist period: no ATMs; no regular gas stations on intercity roads; no reliable hot water; and other than in a few places in the major cities, no decent restaurants and no credit cards accepted. The roads were in terrible condition and the faces of most buildings were heavily scarred by Communist crumble. In the city, signs of poverty could be seen everywhere—signs like little more than the basics for sale in the streets and on nearly barren store shelves; shabbily-clothed people shuffling about in worn-out shoes with mostly struggle and deep worry etched on their faces; and all manner of shysters and thieves swarming about trying to get their hands on your money. The rural areas, with their rudimentary horse-drawn wagons; animals running about; decrepit houses with water wells, outhouses, and wood-and-tar-paper sheds; haystacks everywhere; streets of mud; and people bent over in the fields using primitive farm tools seemed not to have changed since at least the turn of the last century.

An immigrant from Lutsk that my brother found in New York had given us the name and phone number of a Lutsk acquaintance. The acquaintance (Vladislav was his name) turned out to be an ardent Communist who had not yet come to terms with his demotion from party apparatchik to virtual irrelevance—he ranted on and on about how much better off everyone was in Communist days. As Vladislav put it, he had been a Jew before he was an Internationalist. He knew about Trochenbrod, and with pleasure showed us its approximate location on a large regional map in the one-room Lutsk Communist Party Headquarters. He also introduced us to a woman, Evgenia, who was born in Trochenbrod and as a sixteen-year-old had survived the

Holocaust by hiding with her parents in the forest. They eventually were found and protected by partisans. She fell in love with one of the Ukrainian partisans and stayed with him in Lutsk after the war. She told us that a group from the Israeli Trochenbrod organization had set up a monument at the site of Trochenbrod five years earlier. Evgenia asked to come with us on our excursion to Trochenbrod the next day.

The following morning Alex's Lada carried the four of us another twenty-five miles northeast, first on a paved road, then a dirt road, then on a tractor trail through the forest. In a village called Yaromel, near where we knew Trochenbrod's mass graves were located, we found an older man who remembered Trochenbrod. His name was Mikhailo. He wore high boots, a heavy black coat, and a Russian-style winter hat. He stood straight but held a cane. His face was lined with age but filled out and handsome, and he seemed robust, like a peasant who had been both well-worn and well-exercised by a life of hard work. Mikhailo remarked that Trochenbrod's people were Jewish and gentle and trusting, and he remembered well the horrors of the Nazi occupation. He had been waiting over fifty years for someone to ask him about it. I fought back tears that took me by surprise when he said that, and for a few moments I couldn't speak. Walking was hard for Mikhailo—he limped and kept his balance with the cane—but he insisted on going with us into the forest to show us Trochenbrod's mass graves. Mikhailo and Evgenia—two who experienced different sides of the

Holocaust in Trochenbrod—walked ahead, side by side, chatting in Ukrainian.

A few hours later, after visiting the mass grave site, we found ourselves wading through knee-high grasses looking for the site of Trochenbrod itself. Eventually we saw in the far distance first a black speck barely visible against the tree line, and then clearly the Trochenbrod monument, an upright slab of black marble. We ran toward it whooping, arms spread wide as if to embrace a lost relative. The monument had been set up at the north end of town, at the spot where Trochenbrod's largest synagogue was sent up in flame by Nazis after they murdered the last of Trochenbrod's people. Near the monument I noticed a triangle of intersecting trails. That same triangular intersection was prominent on the old Russian map. One of those trails had been Trochenbrod's only street. I looked down a double row of scraggly trees and bushes, and felt a shiver: this had been Trochenbrod. There had been people working, families eating, children playing—a place full of life here. My father was born and raised here. And this place didn't slowly come undone, first one family leaving, and then another: it was cut down.

Alex's Lada was about a mile way, where we had left it as the trail we were driving on began deteriorating into an impassable muddy track. When we got there we found the car hopelessly sunk in mud. Evgenia was tired, so Marvin stayed with her by the car while Alex and I hiked back to Domashiv, the closest village to Trochenbrod, to hunt for a tractor to pull us out. Next to one villager's house we saw a tractor that still had markings of the now-defunct Soviet collective farm that gave it up. We knocked on the door and were welcomed warmly by the present tractor owner, who readily agreed to give us a hand. As he was bringing up buckets of water from the well in his front yard and pouring them into the radiator of his tractor to prepare it for the task ahead, an old toothless man, his father, came running out of the house waving his cane in the air and screaming, "Amerikanski! Amerikanski!" He declared that Ukraine had the richest soil in the world and would be a great nation today, greater than America, if those stinking Communists hadn't ruined everything, forced the villagers to have passports so they couldn't leave the villages, and taken their sons for the army and to work in factories so that now none of them know how to farm. Alex translated, and we smiled and nodded our heads as we backed toward the tractor and hopped on. While the son drove us away, the old man continued his tirade standing in the middle of the village street waving his cane, shrinking into the vanishing point.

We extricated the Lada and started our journey back to Lutsk. By now it was dark. All day I had been captivated by the countryside: gaggles of geese running everywhere in the villages, fields both fallow and flourishing, vast forests, bulrush-bedecked streams weaving back and forth through the low areas, villages and horse wagons and wells and fences that seemed frozen in a long ago time, yellow and green flatlands flowing away to the horizon on one side and ending abruptly at the edge of a forest on another. We were driving slowly along the rough dirt road that led several miles through the forest to the intercity road. No people, no traffic, no lights, no noise except for that made by our Lada. I asked Alex please to stop the car and shut off the engine. We got out and stood for several minutes in awed silence. I looked up and saw a very deep and dark blue sky with billions of shimmering stars and sparkling swirls like no sky I had ever seen before. Tears of happiness began to well up at the wonder of this sight, and I realized that I was looking at the same sky my father had gazed at night after night for the first twenty years of his life.

I was hooked. I had to know more. I had to know more about Trochenbrod. I had to know more about the villages in the area. I had to know more about the land here. I had to know more about the forests. I had to know what life was like in Trochenbrod. Over the next twelve years I returned again and again, usually helped by Alex, and also by Ivan Podziubanchuk, an inquisitive and enterprising farmer in Domashiv who became a good friend. On one trip I studied records in the State Archives in Lutsk; on another I walked the length of Trochenbrod's street just to feel its reach and also to look in the ground for artifacts; on another I visited villages in the region and collected firsthand Ukrainian and Polish memories of Trochenbrod; on another I explored partisan history in the area. On one trip I sneaked onto a Ukrainian air force base, lubricating the way with bottles of bourbon I had brought with me from home, and was surprised to see jet fighters bunkered along the runway as we took off in a tiny canvas airplane I had hired because I had to see from above how the clearing that Trochenbrod had occupied was set among the surrounding forests.

I also collected documents related to Trochenbrod—books, memoirs, maps, college theses, government documents, and photographs. Ivan began uncovering Trochenbrod artifacts in his village and giving them to me on my visits. Eventually, realizing that the few remaining native Trochenbroders were now very old, I hurried around the United States, Brazil, Poland, Ukraine, and Israel videotaping people who had spent their early years in Trochenbrod and could describe what life there was like.

I began my research as a sort of family project, finding out about the particular Jewish *shtetl*[1] that my father came from; I didn't know that my father's home town had historical significance. It wasn't a village as I had first thought, but a town, a bustling free-standing commercial center of over 5,000 people that grew out of an isolated farming village set up by Jews in the early 1800s. It existed for about 130 years. Trochenbrod was unique in history as a full-fledged "official" town situated in the Gentile world but built, populated, and self-governed entirely by Jews, that thrived as a Jewish town until its destruction in World War II.

To be sure, Trochenbrod had those *shtetl* qualities captured with warmth and appreciation by Jewish artists the likes

---

1. Literally, townlet. Typically the Jewish section of an East European town, which functioned almost like a separate Jewish village.

of Sholom Aleichem and Marc Chagall. But because Trochenbrod was relatively isolated, and because the people in Trochenbrod were farmers as well as shopkeepers and tradesmen, those *shtetl* qualities were undiluted, magnified, and connected with the outdoors and a farming way of life unknown in other *shtetls*. Trochenbrod's isolation and total Jewishness gave Trochenbroders a feeling that they were largely in control of their own destiny as a town, away from the shifting laws of prevailing governments. It brought about a relaxed Jewish atmosphere where the Sabbath, Jewish holidays, and weddings were celebrated not just in the town but by the town; it opened space for Jewish entrepreneurial freedom and creativity to an uncommon degree; and it led to a powerful sense not only of family but of community, a community somewhat insulated from what was around it, where everyone knew everyone else and shared their lives, their moral values, their religious values, and their traditions. Trochenbrod's story adds a new dimension to the history of Eastern Europe and Eastern European Jewish life.

When I finally decided to write a book, and gathered together all my notes, taped interviews, historical documents, maps, books, artifacts, and other materials, I was surprised by an outpouring from many families who heard about my project and wanted to help preserve and promulgate Trochenbrod's story. They offered me family photographs, some going back to the 1800s. They also offered artifacts for me to photograph, and informal memoirs in which forebears long gone described their lives in Trochenbrod.

I've been deeply gratified and am grateful to the many people from six countries who contributed material and gladly participated in taped interviews. They made it possible for me to walk Trochenbrod's vanished street and see in my mind's eye the hustle and bustle of people buying and selling and arguing and greeting each other, while children run and play, secure as if among family wherever they were in the town. I could hear solemn melodies from the synagogues and rousing songs from Zionist youth meetings, and the clatter of horse wagons and the calls of peddlers from the villages advertising the goods in their wagons that awaited their Trochenbrod customers. What a gift from all the people who wanted to help me bring Trochenbrod back to life, and what a gift across the decades from that lost town in Ukraine that was Trochenbrod.

The main text of this book comprises four chapters covering successive periods in Trochenbrod's history. Readers who want a clear sense of the geographical relationships among places mentioned in the text may want to scan the maps located on pages x-xi, 5, 57, 77, and 83 before reading. Chapter 4 is followed by an epilogue describing what happened to Trochenbrod and its descendants to this day. Photographs and images of many key figures and locations in Trochenbrod's history are featured in the central photo insert.

I draw heavily on firsthand accounts in the text, but some readers may enjoy reading still more such accounts, so I included them in a section at the end called "Witnesses

Remember." These accounts will add richness to a reader's sense of what life was like in Trochenbrod and the surrounding villages.

I've italicized Yiddish or Hebrew terms in the text. If they are not translated in the text, then the first time they appear they are translated in footnotes. They also appear in the glossary, after the "Witnesses Remember" section, where some translated terms are accompanied by pronunciation help and fuller explanations.

Following the glossary is a chronology that provides the dates for milestones in the history of Trochenbrod and also some contemporary world events for context. After that is a section that lists all the print documents I consulted and tells how those documents came into my hands. It also lists the film, photographic, interview, and other sources that informed my presentation of Trochenbrod's story. Last is the acknowledgments section, in which I list all the people who helped me carry out research and prepare the manuscript for this book, noting the particular help each person provided. The list is organized geographically.

Because of fluid territorial control and the presence of large numbers of Polish, German, Russian, Ukrainian, and Yiddish speakers in that part of the world, often called the "Borderlands," any place name can have many variations. To keep things simple I've chosen one name to use in the text for each place, and stuck with it. Usually I use the name that was common in Trochenbrod during the interwar period.

THE HEAVENS
ARE EMPTY

Chapter One

THE FIRST
HUNDRED YEARS

H e lay crumpled in the street, dead, my grandfather. He had been among the determined few who brought comfort and food to families suffering in the epidemic. Soon enough he contracted the disease himself.

As World War I slowly began moving toward its conclusion, a typhus epidemic arrived in Trochenbrod. People had been weakened by years of hardship and suffering brought by the war, and now they were succumbing to the epidemic. The danger of infection kept almost everyone from visiting the miserable households of the sick. My grandfather, Rabbi Moshe David Beider, loved Trochenbrod's children. He brought treats to them in the stricken households, played with them, and read to them with an air of normalcy that gave them hope.

Trochenbrod's street was a broad, straight, dirt path running north and south, nearly two miles long. It was lined on both sides with houses, shops, workshops, and synagogues. Behind each house the family's farm fields stretched back about half a mile to forests on the east and west sides. On wet fall evenings like the one when my grandfather died, Trochenbrod smelled of mud and manure and hay and leather, of potatoes cooking and smoke from woodstoves and pine from the forest. When Rabbi Beider collapsed, an early light snow had begun to fall, a snow that dusted the houses and the people trudging home, and reflected their outlines in the dim light of candle lanterns hanging from trees that lined the street. It was dusk. Except for the sound of a mother calling her child to dinner and the faint murmurs of evening prayer in the synagogues, Trochenbrod was quiet.

— —

What happened at the very beginning? How did this unusual little town of Trochenbrod get its start? There are no founders' documents, no formal records, no photographs. Even the hand-written running historical account said to have been maintained by successive Trochenbrod rabbis was lost in a synagogue fire between the wars. There is no way one can be absolutely certain about anything. Although interviews

I conducted with native Trochenbroders and the memoirs of others that had passed away yielded stories handed down about the first settlers, the stories were far from consistent. I found, though, that I could stand those stories against the facts of Russian history, Eastern European history, tales still circulating among villagers in the Trochenbrod area, even against the lay of Trochenbrod's land today, and piece together the truth, or as close to the truth as we can come.

In the late 1700s, corruption within Poland[1] and a succession of land and power grabs by neighboring countries led to three partitions of Polish territory. In the last of these partitions, in 1795, the Kingdom of Prussia, the Austrian Empire, and the Russian Empire fully divided Poland's territory among themselves, and Poland ceased to exist as a sovereign nation. Russia took Poland's lands east of the Bug River, and these lands, with their sizeable Jewish population, became part of Russia's Jewish Pale of Settlement. With some exceptions, Jews in Russia were allowed to live only in the Pale of Settlement, which had been established a few years earlier by Czarina Catherine the Great. The Czarina's thinking was that by restricting Jews to a defined area, Czarist governments could work their will on them more effectively, and could prevent the Jews from infiltrating Russian society and perhaps even coming to dominate the budding Russian middle class. The Pale stretched from the Baltic Sea to the Black Sea and was home to between five and six million Jews.

1. More precisely, the Polish-Lithuanian Commonwealth.

In the early 1800s, Czars Alexander I and Nicholas I issued a series of decrees defining and then redefining and then redefining again the place and obligations of Jews in the Russian economy and society. They forced rural Jews, already constrained to the Pale of Settlement, to move from the villages and small towns where they lived to the larger towns and cities of the Pale. There government functionaries could more easily monitor, control, tax, and conscript them. Jews could not own land, and rural Jews were merchants, tradesmen, and craftsmen, not farmers.[2] They arrived in the cities largely without resources, and many became destitute because they could not practice their rural trades there. The decrees also denied Jews basic civil rights like equality in the court system and education, and imposed heavy taxes on them. But the decrees exempted from their oppressive measures Jewish families that undertook farming on unused land. Not too many Jews were likely to take advantage of this half-hearted effort to put more land under cultivation, since Jews knew nothing about farming, and chances were that unused land was the land least suitable for farming. Yet the decrees made Jews want to stay as far away from the Czarist government as possible, and rural areas were the best place to do that.

2. There were some rare exceptions, where Jews farmed land they had purchased in the name of a non-Jewish collaborator. Jews generally had not been farmers for nearly two thousand years. The explanations scholars give for this include government prohibitions on Jews owning land, government or local cultural occupational restrictions, the higher return to Jewish literacy investment that could be obtained from urban trades and professions than from farming, and conflict between Jewish religious practice and the demands of agriculture.

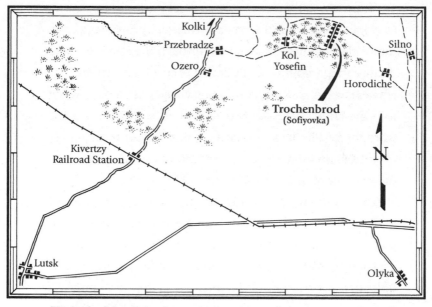

Trochenbrod–Lutsk Area

The historic province of Volyn[3] is today the northwest corner of Ukraine. When Volyn became part of the Russian Pale of Settlement after the 1795 partition, it already had a rich Jewish history going back more than eight hundred years. To evade the anti-Semitic provisions of the new decrees, in 1810, or perhaps a bit earlier, a few Jewish families from the Volyn cities of Lutsk, Rovno, and the much smaller Kolki quietly began homesteading in an isolated spot within the triangle formed by those three cities. They settled in a marshy clearing surrounded by dense pine forests. The land was the property of a local landholder named

3. Also known as "Volhyn" and "Volhynia."

Trochim, who was no doubt happy to let the Jewish settlers try to extract value from the otherwise useless property. A creek tumbled out of the forest and ran through the clearing before disappearing into the woods again. There was a shallow spot where travelers on a trail connecting villages in the area would ford the creek. The place was known as Trochim Ford. The word for ford in Russian is *brod*. To the Yiddish-speaking settlers, Trochim Brod eventually became Trochenbrod. The first baby was born in Trochenbrod in 1813.

It was extremely hard for the first settlers. Imagine the fathers and sons who went there to prepare the place enough so they could bring their families. They drove their horse-drawn wagons to Trochim Ford wearing their city clothing, unloaded their tools and belongings, gathered wood, lit a fire, and slept under the stars the first night. Wild animals roamed the area, and the Trochim Ford clearing was heavily infested with snakes. Those first settlers must have been terrified by the howls and grunts and slithering noises they heard all night long, even as they were filled with happiness that maybe, just maybe, they really would escape the day-to-day hardships and indignities imposed by the Czarist authorities. The next morning, after morning prayers and something to eat, they must have taken a good look around and wondered, can we really do this? They were city Jews who had been shopkeepers, petty traders, and artisans; they knew nothing about farming. But they pushed on, clearing brush and cutting trees from the forest to make primitive shelters for themselves, and later constructing simple houses for their families. Villagers passing by on the trails gave them farming tips, but they learned how to farm mainly through hard work, privation, and trial and error.

Jewish settlement at Trochenbrod expanded slowly, until in 1827 Nicholas I issued a decree that forced conscription of Jewish boys into the Russian army until age forty-five. The Czarist government saw this as a practical and compassionate way of eliminating the Jewish problem, because obviously after twenty or thirty years in the army isolated from his relatives, the forty-five-year-old man would no longer be Jewish. This decree provided an exemption for Jewish families that settled as farmers and worked unused land. The result in Trochenbrod was a surge of newcomers and, as was finally made possible by Volyn administrative regulations, outright purchase of the land by the settlers.

The land at Trochim Ford had not been settled before because it was almost completely unfit to farm: it was a marshy depression in the forest far from any main roads. It was a clearing amid forest lands because trees could not grow in the low, wet soil there. Although trails crossed the clearing, they led to villages that were miles away through woods and other marshy areas. The isolation of the spot meant that a trip to any market would be long and arduous and dangerous. Farming did not suggest itself as a promising way to make a living in this place. But this was a place that was far away from the Czar and his government operatives, a place where Jews were likely to be left alone. It was a perfect place for Jewish settlement.

Even city Jews knew they could not farm on marshy land, so they dug long drainage ditches that stretched behind their houses along the sides of each family's farm field to the edge of the forest. This was backbreaking work, work that made it possible for the new Trochenbrod families to grow crops, and work that those families could not know would offer a path to life in a distant future then unimaginable. All the while, the settlers observed Jewish law and custom strictly, just as they had in the cities they came from. Slowly the years passed and the settlers began to get the hang of it. These Trochenbroders, among only the handful of Jewish farmers in the world at that time, became known in the surrounding villages for their farming skills.

Even so, the soil was poor and the settlers found it impossible to survive only from crops grown in Trochenbrod. Many of them turned to livestock to supplement their crops, and from that, in time, they developed a thriving trade in leather and leather goods and in dairy products. To give themselves more of a livelihood they also drew on their urban experience and set up small shops and provided skilled trades like carpentry and glazing to Ukrainian and Polish villages in the region. These other villages had remained virtually unchanged farming villages for hundreds of years; Trochenbrod, adapting to its circumstances, set itself on a different course.

In 1835, eight years after his conscription decree, Czar Nicholas I issued a new "Law of the Jews." This one required all rural Jews to be in agricultural "colonies," farming villages recognized by the government, and also required them to have passports and permits to travel from these colonies. The idea was to prevent Jews from setting up as farmers to avoid the conscription and other anti-Semitic laws and then quietly moving back to towns and cities. Trochenbrod was forced to come out of hiding, to become an official colony.

In the mid-1820s, a group of twenty-one Mennonite families left their village of Sofiyovka, seventy miles northeast of Trochenbrod, on the Horyn River. They were moving on because after working hard for over fifteen years, they decided that their agricultural efforts yielded too little in that marshy area. They contracted to settle on land owned by Count Michael Bikovski in a sparsely populated area about twenty miles northeast of Lutsk, and established two small new settlements there. One of the new Mennonite settlements, Yosefin, was set up three miles west of Trochenbrod. The other was just south of Trochenbrod, and was named Sofiyovka, after the village the Mennonites had left. There is no record of the relations between Trochenbrod's Jews and Sofiyovka's Mennonites, but they must have been good because both groups were peaceful and quiet types who tended not to concern themselves with other people's business. About ten years later these Mennonites abandoned their new small villages in order to join relatives in a larger Mennonite settlement in the southern "New Russia" region, where local officials were more welcoming to Mennonites.[4] Yosefin was repopulated by ethnic German families. Families like these, which eventually came to be known as Volksdeutsch, originally moved east looking for good Ukrainian farm land, and became one more ethnic group that lived for generations in Volyn and neighboring areas.

About the time that Yosefin and Sofiyovka Mennonites were leaving their villages, Trochenbrod's elders and the Russian government agreed that Trochenbrod would be designated an official colony so that the Trochenbroders could stay in their village. From now on it would even appear on maps, and official colonies needed Russian names. No one knows exactly how it came about, but Trochenbrod was given the name of the Mennonite settlement that had been immediately to its south, and probably incorporated its territory. From then on everyone, Jews and neighboring Gentiles alike, knew the village, and later the town, as both Trochenbrod and Sofiyovka.

I was in the area recently and, curious to see what local people knew of their pre-war history, asked a villager passing by on a horse-drawn farm wagon if he knew where Trochenbrod was. He tilted his head sideways and looked skyward, stroking his chin with his hand, and repeated the name a few times, struggling to place it. His wife, seated comfortably on the pile of hay behind the driver's bench, began gently whipping him with a stalk of grass as if to prod his memory and muttered "The Jews, Sofiyovka." "Ahh, yes, the

4. Some of these Mennonite families immigrated to the United States in 1874.

Jews, Sofiyovka, Trochenbrod," he shouted triumphantly, "Down that way," and pointed in the right direction beyond the derelict barns and chicken coops of a defunct Soviet-era collective farm.

When Trochenbrod/Sofiyovka became an official colony it was not very big—like some other villages in the area, it probably had thirty to fifty families. But in the case of this strange little village, all of its people, numbering at least 250, were Jewish. By this time Trochenbrod had spawned a new small Jewish village nearby, a sister colony called Lozisht by the Jews, Ignatovka by others. The settlers in Trochenbrod and Lozisht were very close; many were relatives. People commonly thought of the two villages as one larger settlement, and many of their descendants think of them that way even today.

Other Jewish farming colonies were established, especially in the mid 1800s and especially in "New Russia," today southern Ukraine. These villages were established for the same reasons that Trochenbrod had been established, but they occupied land that was better for agriculture than Trochenbrod's land. Many of them eventually disappeared because their people could not survive from farming, or tired of it, or returned to towns and cities when eventually the edicts that had motivated their families to become

---

5. The few remnants of Jewish farming colonies that still operated in this area after the Soviet Union was created were absorbed into Soviet collective farms and not heard from again. I found no record of any operating in what became eastern Poland between the wars.

farmers no longer applied.[5] Trochenbrod alone continued to grow and prosper and diversify as a Jewish town and regional commercial center.[6]

Trochenbrod houses were typical of the agrarian Ukrainian style: rectangular, dirt floors, wood-framed stucco walls that were whitewashed, thatched roofs that sloped toward the long sides of the houses, and often window frames with carved wood patterns that stood out quaintly against the stucco walls. The front third of many houses, the part facing the street, was the all-purpose room for sitting and special meals. If the family had a workshop or a business, the space might be adapted to accommodate that activity. A front door opened into that room. In the middle section of the house were two bedrooms: a narrow corridor ran alongside them connecting the front room with the kitchen room at the back of the house. On the side of the house, toward the back, was a second door that opened into the kitchen room—this is where people ate most of the time, much as people do everywhere today.

6. Beginning in the late nineteenth century, in response to pogroms in the Pale of Settlement, the German-French philanthropist Baron Maurice de Hirsch and his Jewish Colonization Association supported transportation of Jews from Russia to new Jewish agricultural settlements they established in Argentina, Canada, and elsewhere in North and South America (also in Palestine). On the whole, these settlements did not survive very long; most of the immigrants or their children moved to urban centers. In one case, however, a settlement named Rivera, in Argentina, does survive today—not as a Jewish town, but as a multi-ethnic town substantially smaller than Trochenbrod was.

The kitchen room had a wood-burning oven and stove that also distributed heat through clay ducts to other rooms of the house. The kitchen typically had a trap door that led to a root cellar, which was used to preserve vegetables for winter meals and also helped preserve dairy foods in summer. Behind the kitchen room, in the backmost part of the house, was a walled-off section that sheltered the animals and opened onto the family's farmland. Above, for all or a part of the length of the house, was an attic, most often used for storing hay. Each house also had an outhouse and a shed in back. This basic homestead model continued to serve many Trochenbrod families, especially the poorer ones, well into the twentieth century.

The single street that ran the length of Trochenbrod was little more than a broad muddy path. To drain the street as much as possible, the townspeople dug drainage ditches along its sides and laid planks across the ditches to make bridges to their homes. The early settlers soon began planting willow trees along the street, probably because willows help protect against erosion, but also to add life and color and shade in the summer. For the generations that followed, and for the sons and daughters of the town who later emigrated abroad, those trees lining the street were a prominent part of the image of Trochenbrod they held in their minds. To this day the site of Trochenbrod's street remains marked by a double row of willow trees and bushes.

The Jews of Trochenbrod were Hasidic Jews.[7] In an 1850 decree the Czarist government outlawed Hasidic dress. The decree was resisted in Trochenbrod but nevertheless had an impact, and Hasidic dress and the practice of Hasidism itself slowly waned over the decades that followed. Yet the town always remained religiously observant. Even toward the end of the ninety years left to Trochenbrod at this point, when some young people became openly nonbelievers, everyone went to synagogue on Sabbath and observed all the religious holidays. It was required by the heads of families: no family would be shamed by having a son out and about when all the men in the town were at prayer in the synagogues.

At the same time that America's Civil War was ending in 1865, Czar Alexander II promulgated a law allowing Jews to change their status from "farm-villager" to "town-dweller" without giving up their land. This time the idea was to allow Jews to keep their farms and return to cities and towns from which they could move about freely and avoid the permit system for ensuring they lived in their villages. But they had to pay a price: in the towns they would be subject to conscription laws. The conscription laws were no

---

7. Hasidic Judaism, or Hasidism, is a subset of Orthodox Judaism that originated in the mid-1700s in a town just southeast of Volyn province. Hasidism emphasized spirituality and joy as key elements of Judaism, in contrast with the typical emphasis at that time on religious scholarship. Different Hasidic sects organized around specific rabbinic leaders, called Rebbes. Hasidic men usually wore dark kaftans, white shirts, and dark fedoras or large round fur hats. Hasidism gradually became a worldwide subset of Orthodox Judaism, but by the early 1800s it was already the rule among Jews in Volyn and neighboring provinces.

longer universal: now a quota of conscripts was set for each community. Those who were conscripted were still required to serve until age forty-five. The Jews of Trochenbrod figured that if they could convince the government to change Sofiyovka's status from a colony to a small town they could stay in place while avoiding the hated passport and permit system for traveling to and from the cities, where they had relatives to visit and business to conduct. By this time Trochenbrod had begun selling its dairy products in the cities of Lutsk, Rovno, and Kolki.

Trochenbrod's elders petitioned the government and were granted town status, figuring they'd find other ways to avoid conscription. This they did by employing tactics that were widespread in the Pale of Settlement: falsifying or avoiding birth records, hiding their sons or having them flee the town when government agents came looking for conscripts, sending their sons to faraway cities for long periods of yeshiva study, and regularly changing family names, so that every son born would be recorded as a "first-born," exempt from conscription.

Nevertheless, the conscription problem created a dangerous situation for rural Jews. When the obligation to supply a son to the army fell on a wealthy town family, they could hire professional kidnappers to snatch another Jewish boy to serve instead. Gangs of such kidnappers, *chappers* they were called, roamed urban and rural areas looking for suitable targets. Trochenbrod lost a number of young people this way. In his memoir published in Israel in the 1950s,

Trochenbrod native David Shwartz recounts a childhood memory—it must have been at the turn of the century—of a letter arriving from a stranger saying that he was looking for a brother he had not seen in many years. The brother's name was that of David's grandfather. The mysterious letter-writer eventually visited. He looked very much like David's grandfather, they had a tearful reunion, and he stayed with his brother in Trochenbrod for a few days. But he remained a stranger. They could not really connect; there was a gulf of life experience that could not be bridged even by brotherhood. The visitor had been kidnapped by *chappers* as a youngster. He said he was a general in the Russian army and had been baptized, but now he was thinking of fleeing Russia and returning to Judaism. Then he left Trochenbrod and was never heard from again.

By 1880 Trochenbrod was visibly being transformed into a bustling little town. Behind every house there was a kitchen garden and a small farm that supplied the family table and often also provided produce like potatoes and cabbage for market. Many Trochenbrod families also raised livestock for dairy, meat, and hides. Many hired Ukrainians from nearby villages to help with gardening and farming. But bit by bit, as the years went by, Trochenbrod's economy came to be dominated more and more not by farming but by nonfarm enterprises—commerce, craftsmen, workshops, small factories like oil presses and flour mills, and non-agricultural professions like teaching, healing, and kosher slaughtering.

David Shwartz recalls in his memoir some of Trochenbrod's people as he knew them near the end of the 1800s. At this point in Trochenbrod's economic diversification the types of nonagricultural activities tended still to be relatively basic, though beginning to modernize.

> [There was] long-bearded Motty, in summer a house-painter and in winter he worked in my father's tannery; Shmuel Shimon the shoemaker, a very good man, who used to go from house to house to wake people up for prayers; Yosel the teacher; Abe who owned an oil press; Itzik the weaver; Shmerl the *Shochet;*[8] Wolf, another shoemaker; Chaimke the bathhouse keeper; Moshe Motia the tailor; "long" Chuna the butcher; Chaim Yoel the carpenter; Wolf the scribe; Ziviz the midwife; Motke Zirelis the candlemaker; Berel from the feed-mill; Shmuel the healer; Benzion who had a tannery; Shmilike, who owned a tannery, a little synagogue, and a bathhouse; Yaakov Leib the cooper; Hirschke Katzke who kept a bar; Yankel the blacksmith; and Itzy with the nose.

There is a belief, or at least a suspicion among some surviving people born in Trochenbrod—including the only Gentile born there—that the famous humorist and author Sholom Aleichem secretly visited Trochenbrod, and from there drew the inspiration for the characters and *shtetls* he

8. Ritual slaughterer for kosher meat.

portrayed, including the well-known Tevye the Milkman stories and his tales placed in the village of Kasrilevka. One Trochenbrod native dismissed my skepticism about this with an irrefutable, "Sholom Aleichem so perfectly captured the spirit, the way of thinking, the life, the characters, the struggles, the devotion to God of our town, how could he not have seen it with his own eyes?" More than a few people born in Trochenbrod spoke to me of their home town as if it had been a typical Volyn village portrayed by Sholom Aleichem. But many of these now elderly Trochenbrod natives left the town when they were quite young; we can't be certain where their image of Trochenbrod came from.

Certainly Sholom Aleichem captured widespread qualities of Jewish *shtetls*, especially in the late 1800s in the Kiev and Volyn regions of the Pale of Settlement. *Shtetl* is the diminutive for the Yiddish *shtot*, which means "town." A *shtetl* was a relatively insular Jewish community in an exclusively Jewish section of an Eastern European town—essentially a Jewish village within a Gentile town. The qualities of *shtetl* life have been reflected lovingly and with great warmth by many Jewish artists, and introduced widely to Western audiences since the mid 1960s through the musical production *Fiddler on the Roof*. The central themes in *shtetl* life and culture were home and family life; the synagogue, Sabbath, and Jewish traditions; patching together a livelihood from urban commerce and trades; and protecting all that from outside influence, from physical attack, and from oppression by the Czarist regime. These themes certainly were central to life and culture in

Trochenbrod. The circumstances that made Trochenbrod different from all the Kasrilevkas and Anatevkas were that it was a free-standing Jewish town, not part of a larger town that included Gentiles; it was relatively isolated; and most of its townspeople, whatever else they did, were also farmers.

An 1889 census recorded 235 families in Sofiyovka. At that time European Russia was rapidly industrializing. The government was building a branch of the Warsaw-to-Kiev railroad between Kovel, a transportation hub fifty miles northwest of Trochenbrod, and Rovno, a relatively large city and major trading center thirty-five miles southeast of Trochenbrod. The most direct route would bring the railroad tracks along the southern edge of Trochenbrod, and the plans were drawn up that way. Trochenbrod elders didn't like that idea: they worried about the noise, the hulking encroachment of the government and the outside world on their quiet and uniquely Jewish way of life, and the danger to their wandering livestock. Using the argument about danger to their livestock, the elders successfully petitioned Russian officials to place the railroad tracks on the other side of the forest to the south of town—and by doing that, assured Trochenbrod's relative isolation for its remaining fifty years.

To this day a glance at the map shows the Kovel-Rovno railroad line bearing southward unnaturally from Kovel to Kivertzy station northeast of Lutsk; then continuing on its southeast path until it meets up with the Lutsk-Rovno highway about eight forested miles south of where Trochenbrod used to be. From there the tracks follow a path east and then southeast to Rovno and beyond. Kivertzy station was twelve miles from Trochenbrod by unpaved road. Though it took half a day to get there by horse-drawn wagon, it made Warsaw, Kiev, and the world accessible to Trochenbrod. The railroad figured heavily in partisan activities in World War II, since the Nazis made Rovno the administrative center for their Reichskommissariat Ukraine, and, as we'll see later, the forest provided good cover for partisan demolition squads.

According to census data, by the end of the century the combined population of Trochenbrod and Lozisht was over sixteen hundred Jews. The town's population was growing steadily because it was enjoying a relative economic boom. As Trochenbrod passed into the early twentieth century it boasted flour mills, oil presses, long-distance cattle traders, an extensive leather and leather-goods sector, dairies and a flourishing dairy-goods sector, a glass factory that took advantage of the sandy soil and nearby forests, and close commercial relations with markets in the three cities and a number of towns in the region.

Trochenbrod began to have more regular contact with the outside world than before, and its people were becoming more aware of the major military, diplomatic, and political happenings in Europe, and even, to a degree, in the United States. Many Trochenbrod boys and young men studied at yeshivas as far away as Lublin, Lodz, and Mezerich in modern-day Poland, and Vilna in modern-day Lithuania. To deal with administrative issues, like placement of the railroad tracks, Sofiyovka emissaries traveled as far away as Moscow.

Trade interests took some Trochenbrod businessmen to cities hundreds of miles away, to Warsaw, Kiev, and beyond. Jewish newspapers from Warsaw and other Polish cities, carrying news of both the Jewish world and the larger world, now reached Trochenbrod. Emigration from Trochenbrod to the West, especially to the United States, was fairly brisk in the late 1800s and the early 1900s, and the immigrants sent letters home to Trochenbrod about life and events in their new countries.

And so, despite its relative isolation, as the new century began Trochenbrod was entering the modern world step by step. And yet this unique little town called Trochenbrod remained essentially what it always had been: most young men were sent to yeshivas to study Torah; the whole town celebrated weddings; farming activity was central to community life; being a rabbi and a scholar was the highest and most respected achievement; and when a famous rabbi visited from a big city, the whole town went out to greet him, families would compete to have him as their guest, and his visit was celebrated night after night during his stay. And on the Sabbath, Trochenbrod's Jews did no work, lit no fires, bore no burdens. Despite the relentlessly encroaching world, in the whole town of Trochenbrod, Saturday, the Sabbath, remained a day only for peace, rest, and prayer. In Trochenbrod, as was typical of shtetls, everyone lived for the Sabbath. In all the personal accounts that have come into my hands, Sabbath holds a special place in Trochenbrod memories. For example, David Shwartz reminisces in his memoir

about Sabbath in Trochenbrod in the early twentieth century
with obvious wistfulness:

> Each family had a mill in which the wheat was ground
> into flour. From the barley they prepared tasty cereals.
> Each family possessed a wooden mortar, made from the
> stump of a tree and burning a hole in the root. To use
> in this they made a pestle for crushing. The barley was
> put into the hot oven after the bread had been taken out.
> Inside the oven the barley dried and after that it was put
> into the mortar and crushed with the pestle. This work
> was always kept for Thursday so that they would have
> enough crushed barley for the Sabbath meal.
>
> On Friday everyone finished work early and after lunch
> everyone, young and old, would dash to the ritual bath-
> house to take a bath, would then get dressed in Sabbath
> array and would go to the synagogue. In summer it was a
> pleasure to hear the friendly greetings *"Shalom aleichem"*[9]
> and the music of the voices of the fathers and children
> was carried from the synagogues the length of the street
> and would enter into every limb. After supper we would
> sit out on our front steps and breathe in the delightful
> scents of the grass, the blossoms and the pine trees of the
> Radziwill forest. We had no electric light but there was
> light in our hearts and our eyes sparkled and illuminated
> the darkness around. We used to sleep soundly and
> peacefully without fear of burglars or thieves.

9. "Peace upon you," a traditional Jewish greeting.

On the Sabbath morning one would awaken to the sounds, coming through the open windows, of the chanting of psalms or the reciting of the weekly portion of the Torah. Neither did the women stand idle. They had to wait for the Gentile who came to milk the cows on the Sabbath and for the Gentile cowherd who took the cows out to pasture. After the early morning prayers we would drink the tasty chickory from a pot warming on the oven. The milk was well boiled with a thick skin on it. Only then would we put on our *kapotehs*[10] and girdling cords and our prayer shawls with the *tzitzis*[11] tucked into the cords and we would go to the synagogue in whole families, grandfather, father, sons and grandchildren; a whole regiment!

We came home gaily and in high spirits, made *kiddush,*[12] washed (even the very small boys) and smacked our lips over the calves' foot jelly and *chulunt*[13] that only an angel could have baked so deliciously in the oven, and were served with potato pudding ("kugel"), and if there was a piece of stuffed intestine ("kishke") in addition, then it was indeed a Sabbath meal of the first order. After eating the meat out of the *chulunt* and the *tzimmes*[14] we said grace and went to bed.

We were no sooner up than the hot tea, which

10. A kaftan worn for Sabbath and holiday services.
11. Tassels on the corners of prayer shawls.
12. A prayer sanctifying the Sabbath.
13. Slow-cooked stew, a Sabbath specialty.
14. Baked dish of mixed ingredients.

was taken out of the stove, was on the table. Then the whole family would go out for a walk around the fields and gardens to see and take pleasure in the way all was sprouting, growing, and blooming. Only a villager can realize what this means; a town dweller can never understand it. Many would stroll in the Radziwill forest. The children would pick the wild berries with their mouths for, on the Sabbath, it was forbidden to pick by hand because that was defined as work. After the walk the men would go to the synagogue for the afternoon prayers and would return home to "shalosh seudes," "the third meal," a good "borsht" whipped with cream, and again the singing of the *zmires* [Sabbath songs] would resound throughout the townlet. After evening prayers we made "havdala," the ritual prayer differentiating between a holiday and a routine day. The women would then go off to the cow stalls to milk the cows and churn the butter, as it had to be ready for dispatch to Lutsk early on Sunday morning.

Everyone lived for the peaceful routine of the Sabbath, and the year was marked by the Jewish holidays. People gave the date of their birth as so many days or weeks before or after the nearest Jewish holiday. Shmilike Drossner, another pre–World War I immigrant to the United States, had this to say about *Hanukah*, the Jewish "Festival of Lights" holiday, in Trochenbrod:

To tell you how we lit our candles on Hanukah in Trochenbrod, I can tell you as follows, and you will think it is funny. We took ordinary potatoes, cut them in half and made a small hole in each half, and put a little oil and piece of cotton, and then we lit it. The rich probably had candles, but the average person did not have candles and used potatoes instead. The tradition with handing out *Hanukah gelt*[15] and playing with *dreidels*[16] was the same as in this country. Also the tradition of making all kinds of *latkes*,[17] especially raw potato *latkes* which were very popular. It was really a treat, and a lot of work supplying the *latkes* as everyone had good appetites and were not on diets.

About *Sukkot*, or *Sukkos*, the Feast of Tabernacles, the Jewish fall harvest celebration for which families build a small temporary hut for eating outdoors during the seven-day holiday period, Shmilike explained:

Everybody had a *sukkah* [temporary hut], which they made with their own hands. But our grandfather, Yuda Meir, had one that was sort of stationary, and it was only necessary when *Sukkos* came to put the finishing touches on it. Most of the time we froze in there, as the cold weather started earlier in Trochenbrod than here. Some of the *sukkahs* were so frail (they were made from corn stalks) that some of the animals such as cows, etc., would

15. Coins given to children during the Hanukah holiday.
16. Spinning top used for Hanukah games.
17. Potato pancakes, a traditional Hanukah dish.

push in the walls and cause damage. In spite of all this, we enjoyed the holiday.

Baking *matzah*, the unleavened flatbread eaten during Passover, was a complicated matter at that time, according to Shmilike:

I want to explain how *matzahs* were baked in Trochenbrod. The people in Trochenbrod rented a house [in the town] for four weeks before Passover. Then they started to clean it thoroughly to make sure it was kosher. Then each family bought flour enough for their family and they hired girls and women to do the work. One man took care of the oven, and when one family's *matzah* supply was baked it was carried in a bag made of linen hung from a long post and was delivered that way. Then they started on someone else's *matzah*, and so on, until they had baked enough for everybody. This isn't as simple as it may seem. The water that was used in mixing the flour was brought in before it got dark, for the next day, and it was then put in a barrel. It was brought up from a well, one bucket at a time.

You didn't ask about the Passover wine, but I will tell you anyway. Everybody made their own wine of raisins.

About the Passover horseradish and also potatoes, they were grown in our own backyard and we had enough to use all year and also to share with others that didn't have any. They were of the finest quality, the best in our town.

Morris Wolfson came to America from Trochenbrod in 1912. His account offers another window into life in the town as it flowed on the currents of expansion of the late 1800s into the early 1900s.

Every day my father, Wolf Shuster, labored over the shoes he made, and once every two weeks he went the twelve miles to the regional market in Kivertzy, where he sold his shoes to Gentiles. My family owned a cow that gave us milk. The cow, chickens, ducks, and produce from the vegetable garden made us almost self-sufficient. Every house had a garden that stretched back to the woods.

The three hundred or more Jewish families of Trochenbrod (there were no Gentiles in our town) lived almost completely separate from the Christians. The train that stopped twelve miles from our town was our only way to reach faraway places. And this was a luxury few of us could afford. One of my earliest memories was my first time out of our town when I was about four years old. I was sick, and since of course we did not have a doctor in our town I was taken on a train ride to Kiev to see one there.

Every boy attended *cheder* [Jewish day school] from ages four through thirteen, in Trochenbrod. Starting in the early morning we sat and studied Jewish books all day on hard benches made from wood. We didn't come home until after dark. We studied Hebrew, the Talmud, things like that. Our teacher wasn't really a rabbi, but a *melamed* [learned teacher]. We didn't learn modern Hebrew in the *cheder,* that was left to the rabbi. We only needed to know enough Hebrew to read the Torah and the Talmud.

Even though our studies and work and learning our father's trade made us grow up quickly, we still had a childhood. Our toys were simple homemade toys. We used to play in the fields. We tried to catch birds. We would make a certain little trap and set it in the field to catch the birds. Of course we would get the birds with the idea of holding it and then letting it fly away.

In our town we spoke Yiddish. To the Gentiles we spoke Russian and Polish. Probably more Polish, because Trochenbrod was so close to the border, many villages in the area had Polish-speaking peasants. We used the languages of the Gentiles when we did business with them.

A wedding was a joyous event in Trochenbrod; everyone participated. I remember that marriages were arranged by the fathers without the children's permission. Two fathers would meet in the field. "If I'm not mistaken," one says, "you have a girl sixteen years old and my boy's seventeen. I think they would be alright." After deciding on a dowry which could be money or food and board at the bride's parents' house for a certain amount of time, the fathers shook hands and this way decided their children's fate. At the wedding everyone danced, men with men and women with women. Meanwhile the nervous bride and groom sat at the ends of the long table and looked at each other wondering what would be. Despite what each one thought, the match was accepted.

There were no Tzeitels, no refusals, and no Chavas, no intermarriages. Not in our town. [Tzeitel and Chava are two of the daughters in *Fiddler on the Roof*.]

Until I was ten years old, when they used to say the word Jerusalem, or Yerushalaim, I had no idea that it even existed in this world even though I went to *cheder*. I thought it was something on top of a mountain in heaven. The only outside thing that everyone knew about was America, the land of opportunity. We were aware only that things were good in America. Everybody wanted to get out and go there where everyone did alright. We thought that the sidewalks were made of gold. America was our goal and how to get there was our major problem.

In the early twentieth century, as the world moved inexorably toward World War I and Russia moved inexorably toward the Bolshevik Revolution, ideological currents coursing through Europe began to seep into Trochenbrod. Communist, Labor Zionist, Beitar (a right-leaning Zionist youth organization that stressed self-defense), General Zionists, and other secular movements sprouted in the town. Trochenbrod became somewhat more up-to-date, with a wide assortment of religious, cultural, and social organizations, and an ever-expanding array of businesses. By the time World War I erupted in 1914, many Trochenbroders were regularly visiting the nearby cities several times a year for trade, medical attention, government affairs, to buy things not available in Trochenbrod, to have their photographs taken, or to call on relatives. Trochenbroders knew about and argued about world events and Eastern European and Jewish affairs. The town continued to prosper and diversify in terms of the numbers and variety of economic activities. It increasingly became a commercial center for Ukrainian and Polish villages in the region, even as it managed to remain relatively isolated and deeply religious.

By this time, not only had Trochenbrod's nonagricultural activities diversified quite a bit and prospered, its agriculture had also diversified. The main crop and staple of the Trochenbrod diet was potatoes, as it had always been. But now farmers also grew wheat, rye, oats, barley, and a variety of vegetables—cabbage, radishes, carrots, cucumbers, beans, corn, tomatoes, and beets. They raised cows for milk and other dairy products, and chickens, geese, and ducks for food, for cooking fat, and for feathers to make pillows and bedding. The nearby forests provided blueberries, red currants, and huckleberries, as they do still today. On the whole, because Trochenbrod families lived on the land, they always had plenty to eat, unlike Jews who lived in truly urban towns and cities, who often suffered from hunger. When they could work it out through a friend or relative, Jewish families that lived in the cities in the region sent their marriageable girls to Trochenbrod in the summer for fattening that would make them more desirable.

David Shwartz wrote,

> In autumn the potatoes and beans were harvested. The potatoes were stored under the beds and the beans in

the lofts. Potatoes for *Pesach* [Passover] and for seed were buried in a hole dug in the garden: on one side those for *Pesach* and on the other the seed potatoes for sowing. The potatoes which were sweetened by the frost were used for baking at *Pesach*. There was plenty of goose-grease (*shmaltz*), and from *Purim*[18] onwards eggs were stored in preparation for *Pesach*. Every householder would fatten geese and turkeys from which he would get enough *shmaltz* for the whole year. In winter, meat was scarce and the main dishes were potatoes and beans. The families were large and they used to make dumplings, puddings, and pancakes, all from potatoes. The city Jews indeed called us the "Trochenbrod Potatoes."

We had all kinds of small factories, workshops, and tanneries. There were shoemakers, tailors, teachers, carpenters, blacksmiths, locksmiths, painters, bricklayers, foresters, brickmakers, sawmills, wheelwrights, feed mills, oil presses, a glue factory, and a glass factory. The Jews made a good living. There were in addition all kinds of stores and shops: glaziers, wood dealers, butchers, cattle dealers, dealers who supplied geese and eggs and dairy products to Lutsk and Rovno and to places as far away as Prussia, and contractors who supplied horses, straw and meat to the army.

There were many Jews also who lived by their land alone and also all the above-mentioned tradespeople

18. Festival of Lots, a happy holiday that falls about a month before Passover.

worked their own fields, either alone or with assistance, in addition to their professional work. Apart from corn and wheat the land produced all. We had to buy nothing apart from bread and meat. The very poor people who did not have enough money with which to buy bread and meat for the Sabbath, made do with potatoes and beans, and each for himself was happy and contented with his life. We lived an organized and wholly Jewish life and we practiced Jewish rituals in accordance with Jewish law.

From the 1880s through the 1930s, except during World War I, Trochenbrod sent waves of immigrants to North and South America, and between the wars to Palestine as well. The earliest mention of an immigrant to the United States in Trochenbrod family histories is 1880. But as was the case throughout Eastern Europe, the largest wave from Trochenbrod was in the first decade or so of the twentieth century. There is a wealth of Trochenbrod family stories and memoirs describing the experiences of immigrants from Trochenbrod in the years leading up to World War I.

For many Trochenbroders, especially young men, there were lots of good reasons for emigrating from Trochenbrod at that time. Stories of unbelievable economic opportunity in America were trickling back to Trochenbrod, while physical expansion to accommodate the children of Trochenbrod families was not possible because the town was hemmed in by forests owned by wealthy Polish gentry who were profiting nicely from the timber. Though Trochenbrod's relative isolation had shielded it from anti-Jewish hooliganism so far, reports of pogroms and anti-Semitic attacks across Russia suggested trouble ahead. Oppressive anti-Jewish regulations were still in effect throughout Russia, such as restrictions on education, employment, business pursuits, and movement; and while Trochenbrod suffered from these restrictions less than most Jewish communities, long-term economic and social prospects under the Czarist government were clearly grim for all Jews. Finally, Trochenbrod's young men were threatened with conscription into the Czarist army during the Russo-Japanese war in 1904 and 1905, so at that time a great wave of them stole the borders and found their way overseas.

Trochenbrod immigrants went to the United States and settled in larger cities like New York; Boston; Baltimore; Cleveland; Pittsburgh; Detroit; Philadelphia; Washington, D.C.; Columbus; and Portsmouth, New Hampshire. In South America, some went to Argentina and some to Brazil, but also to Venezuela and Cuba. In Argentina, the German Jew Baron de Hirsch established a Jewish colony called Rivera not far from Buenos Aires, to which he sent many Russian Jews, including a number of Trochenbrod families, for a better life. Some Trochenbrod immigrants went first to places in South America, to where their travel was paid by sponsors or where they had relatives, and after a period moved to the United States.

In 1910, a rabbi born Moshe David Plesser, who after a child or two had changed his name to Moshe David Pearl-mutter to help his sons evade conscription, accepted a position as the Berezner Rabbi in Trochenbrod. He came from the town of Verba, about forty-five miles south of Trochenbrod, where his father was a rabbi and scholar descended from a long line of rabbis well-known in the Volyn region. A follower of the Berezner Hasidic sect, Moshe David jumped at the chance to relocate to the town that was now known among Volyn Jews as a place where, incredibly, being a Jew meant being what everyone else was. The Berezner synagogue was located toward the southern end of Trochenbrod on the west side of the street, and Rabbi Moshe David Pearlmutter moved into the house next door with his wife Bella and their eight children. In 1912 Bella gave birth to their ninth and last child, a son they named YomTov—holiday, a day of happiness. In order to have this child, too, recorded as a first-born ineligible for conscription, Moshe David, my grandfather, again changed the family name, this time to Beider.

In an article written in 1945 in Palestine by an immigrant from Trochenbrod, Moshe David Beider is remembered as the Chief Rabbi of Trochenbrod, though there was no such formal title, highly regarded by the townspeople. He was "a great scholar and very educated in matters of the wider world," and was an ardent Zionist. He was known as a very personable man who was attentive to the needs of the people of Trochenbrod and had a special affection for its children.

World War I brought devastation and hardship to Trochenbrod, as it did to much of Europe. As the front between the Habsburg Austrian troops and Russian troops shifted back and forth through the area around Trochenbrod there was intense fighting and widespread destruction. The glass factory and several other small factories were destroyed, livestock were confiscated, homes and shops were looted, and remittances stopped arriving from relatives who had emigrated abroad. The economy of Trochenbrod was decimated; the people were terrorized and brutalized.

In late 1915, Habsburg Austrian troops pushed out the Russians, under whom Cossacks had been allowed to ransack Trochenbrod, pillaging, raping, and murdering. When the Austrians occupied Trochenbrod they at first requisitioned all food to feed their troops, returning only scraps to the townspeople, and they imposed forced labor, requiring everyone to cook or wash or sew or make leather goods or tend horses or in some other way support the army, even on the Sabbath. During the nine months of Austrian occupation Rabbi Beider continued his teaching programs for the children in order to give them structure and routine and purpose as best he could. At the same time he cultivated a good relationship with the Austrian commandant, with whom he was able to converse in German and discuss world events. He convinced the commandant that productivity would increase if he allowed the people of Trochenbrod to observe the Sabbath and Jewish holidays, have a more reasonable workload at other times, and improve their nutrition. As a result of Rabbi Beider's diplomacy and the relative civility of the Austrian troops, the Jews of Trochenbrod considered that they had been treated better under the "Germans" than the Russians. The memory of this later served them poorly during World War II.

As the war wound down and Trochenbrod began the long process of recovering and rebuilding, the town was left in the hands of the Russians. In 1917, the year of the Bolshevik Revolution, the typhus epidemic rippling through Eastern Europe struck Trochenbrod. After suffering years of hardship during the war, the people of Trochenbrod yielded easily to the disease and were strained to their limits to care for ill family members. Terror and despair were in everyone's eyes. Anguished parents looked on helplessly as rashes spread over their children's skin, they began violently coughing and vomiting and crying out in agony, and finally coughed up blood and surrendered their exhausted bodies. Authorities boarded up the homes of families where typhus struck, believing that would help check the disease. Rabbi Moshe David Beider, too, was struck by the infection. On a damp fall night, as an early light snow fell and he was stumbling home from the house of an ailing family, my grandfather collapsed in the street and died.

Chapter Two

BETWEEN THE WARS

The devastation of World War I put an abrupt end to the rise of Trochenbrod's star, its rapidly diversifying businesses and growing prosperity, its increasing weight as the regional center of economic gravity.

Shaindeleh Gluz was born in Trochenbrod in 1913, but in the informal memoir she wrote in 2002 she remembered life there during the war years vividly:

> My paternal forefathers were glass blowers. When the glass factory was gone my grandfather became the

mayor, tax collector and postmaster of Trochenbrod. He also had a butcher business. My father Zrulik and his brother Itzak ran it.

Grandma and some of her family left for America in 1914, just as I was starting to crawl. There was a lot of unrest in the world. There were rumors of war, and suddenly it happened; war was declared. All avenues of communication ceased. World War I was for real, it was on. There was no way to escape . . . no more elaborate plans to migrate. Immigration was stopped, there was no mail, no communication . . . only pain and suffering.

The invading army confiscated money, jewels, silver and all valuables from the town's people. When the war was finally over, the fighting ceased in our town. All the plundering and killing was over. The young girls came out of hiding, no more rapes, no more deaths of the innocent. The commanding officers and their entourage withdrew from Trochenbrod. My grandfather's home had been stripped of all furnishings that had been in the family for generations, but we were alive.

The war had taken its toll on my parents, especially my mother. She was very sick. She was always in bed. Things inside of our house weren't clean and didn't shine any more. It didn't smell sweet and good. The aroma of cooking was also gone. Our clothes were torn and neglected. There was little food in the house. Often we were hungry. Mother was too weak to improvise any meals with the little bits of scraps that we had. Most of the time my little brother Yossel and I stayed in bed with Mother to keep warm, but we were so hungry.

Once in a while, while in bed with Mother, Yossel and I would play a game, "Lets Pretend," with a large collection of well-worn colorful picture post-cards. The cards were of the Statue of Liberty and the teeming Lower East Side of New York. Mother's family sent the cards to us when they settled in America. From these pictures, Mother would weave wonderful tales of freedom, peace, happiness and plenty.

Shortly after Mother passed away, many more sad happenings began. My little brother Yossel and my father became very ill. Yossel and I shared a tiny bed. One morning my little brother's body was cold and stiff. His little life was snuffed out before he had a chance to live. He died of smallpox. I suppose that Yossel's death really caused father's complete breakdown, healthwise, and his death.

There came a time when we really didn't have a piece of bread to eat. We foraged in the woods for berries and sour grass. Our bellies became swollen. We found ourselves too weak from hunger, too sick with festering body sores and lice to give a care anymore. We just couldn't go on anymore. Make no mistake; we were not alone in this situation. All of Trochenbrod was suffering. We became like animals; we hunted for scraps of food; like animals we fought cunningly to survive.

Just when the struggle became too much to bear, when we were ready to succumb to the unknown, fate intervened and help came. One day Trochenbrod was seething with excitement. Since the war was finally over, the ban on traveling had been lifted. The first person to arrive was a rich American. He had been commissioned by concerned relatives in America to go to our town and seek out their relatives. With him he brought letters and money for some of the people. He was also asked to help some of the townspeople to make their way to America. My brother and I reached the center of town just in time to hear the American call our names.

The Austro-Hungarian Empire, also known as the Habsburg Empire, finally collapsed in 1918. But the Treaty of Versailles signed at the end of World War I did not concretely define the border between the reconstituted Poland and the newly constituted Soviet Union. Immediately, Poland and the Soviet Union took up arms over control of the borderlands area that included Trochenbrod. Again the front moved back and forth through the area. Again Trochenbrod was ravaged. When the Polish were the occupying force they expressed their loathing of Jews in the form of beatings, forced labor, looting, raping, and confiscation of food. When the Soviets were the occupying force they preferred to confiscate property from wealthier people, take over businesses, and hunt for imagined Polish spies. The fighting in this secondary war finally ended in 1920, and in 1921 the Treaty of Riga that divided the borderlands between Poland and Soviet Russia was signed. This is when Shaindeleh Gluz heard her name called in the center of Trochenbrod, and then made her way to the United States. Trochenbrod was now in Poland.

— —

For this period of Trochenbrod's history there is a great deal of source material—though never enough, and some of it contradictory. I found good maps; hand-written Sofiyovka civic records; directories that included Trochenbrod survey information and descriptions; memoirs; and references to Trochenbrod, usually brief references, in several books. Sources like these made it possible for me to draw the physical, commercial, and human outlines of Trochenbrod in the interwar years, but not the content within those outlines. What did the street look like? How did the people dress? How did the ways Trochenbroders made their living affect community life? What were the relations like between rich and poor? How did the Jewishness of the place express itself? What did the kids do in the summer? In short, what was the feel of the interwar Trochenbrod, this "last" Trochenbrod? What was it like to live there?

I was lucky to fall under Trochenbrod's spell at a time when a few dozen people who knew Trochenbrod first-hand were still alive. I talked with people born there from 1912 through 1932, and who left as late as 1942. I was able to hear a different perspective, how Trochenbrod and Trochenbroders appeared to Ukrainians and Poles living in other places in the area, from people who still live there and remember well their childhood visits to Trochenbrod. Personal recollections, as unreliable as any one of them might be, collectively made it possible to fill the outlines with the feel of Trochenbrod, with a sense of what was it like to live there. My father left Trochenbrod in 1932; I was capturing things he would have told me.

Trochenbroders usually went to Lutsk, about 20 miles and the better part of a day's journey away, for studio photographs, or had photographs made by itinerant photographers who from time to time set up temporary studios in Trochenbrod. This explains why you can look through hundreds of photographs from Trochenbrod and see the faces of its people, most often stiff and posed, and nothing of the town's physical appearance. By the 1930s box cameras and 35mm cameras were readily available, and at least some people who visited Trochenbrod, usually immigrants returning to visit their families, snapped outdoor photos. Some Trochenbroders had cameras also, but their photographs were lost in the Holocaust. The one Trochenbroder who was technologically attuned, who photographed outdoor scenes, and survived the Holocaust with her photographs and other personal belongings was the Polish Catholic postmistress of the town, Janina Lubinski. I met her son, Ryszard Lubinski, in the city of Radom, two hours south of Warsaw, and with happiness he gave me most of the photos of 1930s Trochenbrod that appear in this book. They add a layer of concreteness to Trochenbrod like nothing else can; they allowed me to see the town my father grew up in.

When my father marked his bar mitzvah in the early 1920s, the combined population of Trochenbrod and Lozisht was the same as it had been twenty years earlier, about sixteen hundred people. Emigration, disease, and war privation had offset any natural growth. The first few years after the wars were a period of harsh life and recovery. In the early days of full Polish administration, local commandants imposed forced labor on the Jews of Trochenbrod—building roads, administration buildings, and warehouses in the region; supplying the Polish army with food, clothes, and leather goods; hauling construction materials and army supplies; building furnishings for government offices. That hardship was soon replaced with higher-level official discrimination. Government jobs were denied to Jews. Some trades that Jews had been prominent in, such as vodka and salt, were made state monopolies and turned over to Polish Catholic war veterans to operate. Systematic repression of Jews steadily increased throughout the interwar period. So did regular outbreaks of violence against Jews, and these were ignored if not encouraged by Polish officials. Despite this, and because people in the rural areas tended to get along better than in the cities—Poles, Ukrainians, and Jews each having their own social and economic niches—Trochenbrod's economy again began to grow and diversify.

Although increased contact with the outside world and a measure of political awareness had come about in Trochenbrod to some extent during the end of the nineteenth century into the early twentieth century, World War I and the Polish-Soviet war pushed the town on a faster path to modernity—technological, commercial, cultural, social, and political. During the wars Trochenbrod had rubbed up against Russian, Austrian, Polish, and Soviet troops. Some young men had fled to distant cities to avoid the troubles in Trochenbrod or to attend yeshiva, and they returned more worldly wise; some had been taken into the military and were exposed to a secular world and nonkosher food. This all laid the groundwork for a Trochenbrod that during the interwar period had growing ranks of secularists, political movements from the far left to the far right, and businessmen whose enterprises reached out to the larger world.

I do not mean to overstate the case: Trochenbrod remained surrounded by forests, far from any reliable transportation route for motorized vehicles, and completely and somewhat insularly Jewish. It continued to be a town, a complete town, governed by Jewish custom: always observing the Sabbath and Jewish holidays, always strictly kosher and following Jewish dictates, always filling up its synagogues, and always greeting visiting Jewish scholars with celebrations. For Jews who knew about the town and for most who lived there, this, together with its farming character, lent Trochenbrod an out-of-place and out-of-time almost magical quality.

As the 1920s gave way to the 1930s, Trochenbrod was thriving again. Its economy was increasingly becoming the center of trade, artisans, agroprocessing, and light manufacturing for a region stretching over a radius of more than ten miles. Much has been made, and rightly so, of the uniqueness of Trochenbrod's Jewish farmers at that time. One of the most eloquent expressions of the wonder of this was written by the Israeli writer Jacob Banai in his 1978 book *Anonymous Soldiers*:

> Sofiyovka is the name of a small Volyn town in which in the fall of 1938 the first *Etzel*[1] course took place, in which I participated. The Jews led their lives in Sofiyovka as if it was their kingdom. That is where I first encountered Jews who worked in agriculture. In Sofiyovka I saw Jews walking behind their plows; a Jew who takes his cows to the field, and when the time for prayer has arrived he stands in his field and prays as if he is standing in a synagogue.
>
> That picture deeply ingrained itself in my memory, and it was the first taste I had of our vision of a Jew in his homeland. I also saw children there, not organized in any activities, but actually small children playing in the fields, dancing and singing Hebrew songs. What a magical place was this Sofiyovka!!!

Memories like this, perhaps reinforced by what lingered in the minds of children who left Trochenbrod at a very young age, and also the memoirs of people who left Trochenbrod well before World War I, have given many today the notion that Trochenbrod was essentially a farming village. In fact, by the 1930s, and perhaps well before that, no one in Tro-chenbrod actually made their living from farming. Although

1. Jewish paramilitary organization fighting for a Jewish state in Palestine.

everyone worked their land to some degree, the livelihoods of most Trochenbrod families, or by far the larger part of them, now came from retail shops, leather-related businesses, construction trades, small-scale manufacturing, and trading.

By now, growing numbers of Ukrainians and Poles from surrounding villages were employed in the town's fields, houses, and sometimes even businesses. It became more and more common for people from surrounding villages not only to shop in Trochenbrod but also to sell things there house to house or from their wagons. Trochenbrod was, as before, one long street with houses, shops, workshops, small factories, and synagogues, but now also with public buildings like schools, a cultural center, the post office, and the constable's office lined up along it. Many houses had already been rebuilt or were now being rebuilt, improved, and enlarged; and now most shops had their own storefronts and carried an ever-increasing variety of goods. As it embarked on the 1930s, Trochenbrod had become truly a regional town.

One sign that this was happening is the town's appearance in Poland's first official "Illustrated Directory of Volyn," published in 1929. The directory listed only places that were economically or touristically significant, and Trochenbrod was considered one of those. The entry for Sofiyovka reads,

> Eleven kilometers east of Trostjanetz is Sofiyovka. It is an industrial town. . . . The easiest access route by rail is through the Kivertzy station (22 kilometers). The main industry is leather–working, and there are over 20 small

leather workshops. In addition there are many Jews there; they are farmers. The town is built on pilings on swampy land, and during the spring snow-melt the water rises to the floors of the houses. There is a new and size-able wooden church, built with pine and oak, funded by the Radziwills.

Yes, a church! More on this later.

Also in 1929 there was an entry for Sofiyovka in *Księga adresowa Polski,* a privately published Polish business direc-tory. The entry listed about ninety nonfarm businesses in Sofiyovka in a wide variety of sectors that included shops, workshops, small factories, and traders. Next to each type of enterprise appear the names of the proprietors of those businesses. Many prominent Trochenbrod family names show up there—names that today are spread throughout North and South America and Israel, and also throughout this book: Antwarg; Blitzstein; Bulmash; Burak; Drossner; Fishfader; Gelman; Gilden; Gluz; Halperin; Kerman; Kessler; Potash; Roitenberg; Safran; Schuster; Shpielman; Shwartz; Szames; Wainer. In this *Księga adresowa Polski* entry the only distinctly Polish names in the long list of Sofiyovka business proprietors are those who run the government-monopoly vodka and tobacco shops.

The breadth of enterprises in this town as early as 1929 may be surprising at first, considering the extent of physical and personal devastation suffered there in the wars. But after having recovered in basic physical terms, stabilized in human terms, and settled into the idiosyncrasies of the Polish administration, around the mid 1920s Trochenbrod had begun to reclaim its place as a regional commercial center with renewed energy. And while some Trochenbrod families never recovered the economic well-being they enjoyed before World War I, and some now even scraped along mostly with the help of money sent by relatives who lived abroad, as the 1930s got under way, many Trochenbrod families were beginning to do relatively well and saw that a comfortable future might be possible in their town.

It's a safe guess that a policy of economic diversification in order to promote growth and stability in Trochenbrod never crossed the mind of anyone who lived there. But, willy-nilly, that is what happened. Diversification of economic activity is a time-honored family strategy, especially among rural families, to pin down a dependable stream of income. Add to that the unusual range of economic opportunities presented by involvement of Trochenbrod families in both agriculture and town businesses, an entrepreneurial heritage handed down from urban roots, and a potential market that included a dozen or more villages in the area, not to mention three cities, and you have the formula for a community of people who would discover and seize a wide variety of economic opportunities. And once they seized one they immediately began to build on it.

A good example of this was Moishe Sheinberg. Moishe was somehow involved in the butcher business in Trochenbrod when he noticed that, like Jews, Polish people for some reason did not eat the hind quarters of cows. He figured that there must be lots of castoff cow rumps he could sell to Ukrainians. Indeed there was. He was able to buy these parts relatively cheaply and then sell them at market in Kivertzy. Moishe was, of course, strictly kosher: he would never eat the nonkosher meat he sold.

Then there was Avrum Bass. Avrum was a farmer who sold his produce at market, and had a horse and wagon to transport his goods. He would often bring produce back from the market in his wagon to sell in Trochenbrod, so he became both a farmer and a produce trader. His familiarity with horses led him to sell the one he had and buy another, and before long he was also a horse trader. Sometimes he brought bread back from the market to sell in Trochenbrod. Why not bake it here and offer fresher bread that people from the nearby villages might also come to buy? Soon enough, Avrum Bass was a relatively well-to-do businessman who grew and traded produce, was a trader in horses, and owned a bakery in Trochenbrod.

Dairy owners in Trochenbrod took their milk and butter to Lutsk, Rovno, and Kolki to sell. Why come back with empty wagons? They began bringing back sugar, cooking oil, and eventually a wide variety of other goods from the cities to sell in Trochenbrod. They expanded their dairy shops into grocery stores and thought of themselves not just as dairymen but also as grocery shopkeepers and traders in city goods.

Ellie Potash started out making shoes and selling them in

his small Trochenbrod shop like so many others. To get an edge on the competition he bought a horse and wagon and made rounds in the villages to take orders from customers and sell shoes directly to them. People would ask him for other leather goods, especially boots, belts, and bridles. Steadily he expanded his "export" business, and by the mid-1930s had a workshop in its own building (next to the post office) making a wide variety of leather goods for a steady market of customers in the villages around Trochenbrod. He made a good living from this and was able to build a very nice new house. He could not have imagined that just a few years later his house would be selected by the Germans as one of the places to store the belongings of their victims, and then to quarter themselves, while Ellie and his family struggled to survive the winter hiding in the Radziwill forest.

As the entry in the 1929 "Illustrated Directory of Volyn" implied, if there was a single dominant industry in Trochenbrod, it was leather. The leather business included buying skins and buying cows for their skins; tanning; working leather into a wide variety of products, especially boots and shoes; leather goods shops; shoe shops; shoe repair; and exporting leather and leather goods to cities in the area, trading at regional markets, selling from wagons of leather merchandise village by village, and wholesaling to small shops in other villages. The biggest tannery, possibly the biggest business, in Trochenbrod was owned by the Shwartz family and employed seven Trochenbrod workers. David Shwartz, who wrote the memoir from which passages are quoted in the first chapter of this book, was one of the Shwartz family children.

Trochenbrod tanners were known for making regular rounds of the surrounding villages looking for and buying cows with skin that would meet their high standards. Sofiyovka boots were considered the highest quality available anywhere for many miles around because of both the leather and the craftsmanship. The steady demand for boots spawned a large number of shoemakers and shoe shops in Trochenbrod to serve people who came from villages and even towns all around to buy shoes, and especially boots, which were so important in the muddy rural area. There were about forty thriving leather-related enterprises in Trochenbrod by the late 1930s. The town's fame as a center for footwear drew so many customers that eventually even a Bata[2] store was established there, a store where people could buy relatively low-cost ready-made shoes that were brought to Trochenbrod from Bata factories elsewhere.

Other businesses that lined Trochenbrod's bustling street by the late 1930s were:

- Bakeries
- Barber shops
- Beer house
- Building materials

2. Bata is a manufacturer of relatively inexpensive ready-made footwear that it retails through its own international chain of Bata retail stores, a business that thrives even today.

- Butchers—the fattier the meat the more it cost!
- Candy store
- Carpenters
- Cattle traders
- Clothes, ready-made
- Dairies, which bought milk from Trochenbrod families and sold dairy products in local shops and in Lutsk, Rovno, and Kolki
- Dressmakers
- Fabric shops, very popular throughout the region because few people bought ready-made clothes
- General store
- Glaziers
- Grain mills, the largest of which was located on the east side of the street in the far north end of town. It had a motor with different attachments for chopping or grinding a variety of raw inputs. Farmers from throughout the region went there to have their grain milled or their hay chopped into more edible feed for their animals.
- Food, other than produce
- Furniture makers
- Haberdashery
- Hat maker
- Heating system builders
- Herbal remedies

- Horse traders
- House builders
- Ice—the ice was cut from a pond at the far north end of town.
- Inn
- Iron-working
- Lumber mills
- *Matzah*-making (in season)
- Metal products like nails and other small items
- Midwifery
- Oil presses, to which farmers from all around brought their oil seeds to be crushed, and pressed to produce cooking oil
- Pharmacies, called aptekas, run by the local *feltchers*, paramedics who treated minor ailments and injuries. When someone was seriously ill they had to be taken to a hospital in Lutsk or Rovno or even Kiev—lengthy, arduous, and potentially dangerous journeys.
- Produce shops
- Restaurant
- Kosher slaughterer
- Tailors

There was also a slaughterhouse and a bathhouse, although not on the main street.

The heads of many families in Trochenbrod were professional traders who regularly frequented regional markets by horse-drawn wagon. They took their products to places like Olyka, Kolki, and Kivertzy, where there were fixed weekly market days for different kinds of products. Some were produce traders—they sold produce like potatoes and cabbage from the fields of Trochenbrod families and bought produce and food products like flour and sugar to sell in Trochenbrod. Others sold Trochenbrod-made goods, especially leather goods, at these markets. Still others traded in livestock.

Trochenbrod supplied artisans—glaziers, house builders, carpenters, builders of cooking and heating systems, painters, bricklayers, roofers, and other specialists—to villagers as far as fifteen miles away. Fifteen miles was the distance a man could walk from Trochenbrod in a day, and then return to Trochenbrod in a day after the job was completed, and avoid night travel made dangerous by robbers, hooligans, and wild animals.

The commercial breadth of Trochenbrod—the almost dizzying array of economic activities in a relatively small and isolated town, the far-flung trading and artisan connections with other places, and the magnetic pull on buyers and sellers from surrounding villages—often came to mind second after family and friends in the reminiscences of Trochenbroders I interviewed. But it tended to be first in the memories of Ukrainians still living in the area today. For example, the first time I visited, as we were trying to locate the site of Trochenbrod we saw an aged woman bent over, working, in the fields of the neighboring village of

Domashiv. We asked if she could point us toward the site of Sofiyovka. She slowly straightened up from her hoeing and looked at us stern-faced for a moment, as if to say, "Who is this asking me such things?" Then, as if thinking, *Oh, I see you're foreigners looking for that place . . . what a place!* a huge grin broke out across her weathered face and she twisted and pointed. "There," she said, "Keep walking in that direction through the fields on the other side of that grove and you'll see a small black monument that marks the north end of Sofiyovka. If there had been no Germans you wouldn't need to ask, because you'd see it: it would be a city today, bigger than Lutsk."

A fascinating idea to contemplate. If there had been no World War II, what would have been? Could Trochenbrod really have become a city—big stone buildings, a tram system, a network of paved streets with sidewalks, cars everywhere, perhaps a railroad spur at last, fancy restaurants and upscale shops—a completely Jewish city, a Tel Aviv in Poland or Ukraine?

As a thriving town that was rapidly growing by the late 1930s, Trochenbrod now had its own post office, constable station, and other government offices. For a while, not only the constable but also the office of the chief of police for villages in the area was located in Sofiyovka. As the Polish government continued to rationalize its administration in its new eastern lands, it established a formal district headquarters in the village of Silno, a few miles away through the Radziwill forest—a village much smaller than

Trochenbrod. The chief of police relocated there with all other district offices. Local officials reached out to Trochenbrod, the most prosperous settlement in the Silno district, in many ways, especially when it came to taxes.

The Polish government imposed a variety of taxes. For businesses there were permit and turnover taxes. A shop owner, for example, bought and annually renewed a business permit, and then paid taxes on the turnover of the business. Households had to pay into a compulsory government fire insurance program that supposedly covered the costs of fire protection as well as rebuilding. There were excise taxes on matches, liquor, tobacco, kerosene, and other nonfood basics. And then there was the chief of police. In the late 1930s this was a big man: one Trochenbroder described him as over six feet tall and three feet wide. He regularly came from Silno to visit the Sofiyovka part of his domain. He would stop into Trochenbrod shops, reach out his hand to the shopkeeper, and say a friendly "Shalom aleichem." He had come for the police tax: you knew that when you reached out your hand to shake his, there needed to be a few zlotys in it that would not be there when your hand came back. Trochenbrod had all the trappings of a vibrant commercial town.

There was a lot of agriculture in addition to commercial enterprises. Most Trochenbrod families not only drew a good portion of their food from the farm fields behind their houses, they earned a little extra money from their farming. Behind each house was a shed and perhaps a barn and other out-buildings, and then a vegetable garden. Beyond the vegetable garden Trochenbrod families grew beans, potatoes, cabbage, corn, and other fruits and vegetables, and beyond that was a field reaching back as far as the forest to pasture the cows and other animals. This was a pattern similar to the one that had been practiced in Trochenbrod for a hundred years.

Many Trochenbrod families kept cows, and most also kept chickens and other livestock like geese, goats, and horses. Workers of the three dairies in town circulated among the homes each day to buy milk, one of the multiple small sources of income for many Trochenbrod families.

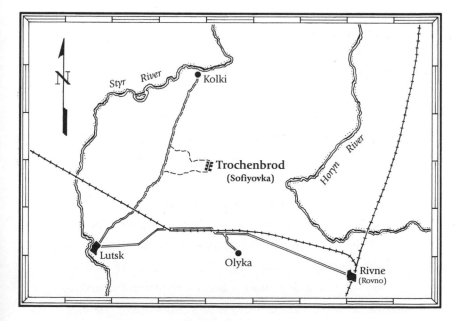

Larger Settlements, Trochenbrod Region

People had close commercial relations with the surrounding towns, and many also had relatives in Lutsk, Rovno, or Kolki. Transportation was improving—the road from the Kivertzy railroad station to Lutsk was now paved, there was limited bus service between Kolki and Lutsk, and both train and bus service were available between Lutsk and Rovno—and many Trochenbroders now frequently traveled to the cities of the region. Basia-Ruchel Potash, Ellie's daughter, was a child growing up in Trochenbrod in the 1930s. She remembers feelings like those of country girls everywhere when they set eyes on the big city:

> I liked to go with my father when he went to the big city, Lutsk, when he went to buy leather and things. He would take me along. I'd look at the buildings and the people and the shop windows and the cars; it was so exciting! I dreamt that when I grow up that's what I'm going to do, I'm going to live in the big city.

Trochenbrod's economic expansion and diversification and extension of its market reach continued at a brisk pace until late 1939, bringing with it more than a doubling of Trochenbrod's population, from sixteen hundred people to over five thousand in Trochenbrod and Lozisht, in the interwar period.

Some of that population growth resulted from people moving to Trochenbrod from surrounding cities because they married into Trochenbrod families; or because it was a uniquely desirable place where one could earn a living, enjoy a rural environment with many city conveniences, and live in a Jewish town; or both. Some of the population growth happened because more people stayed in Trochenbrod than before: it had become more difficult to gain entry as an immigrant to many destination countries, including the United States, and now as more of a commercial center than an agricultural settlement the fixed acreage of Trochenbrod did not limit livelihood opportunities the way it had in earlier generations. And some of the population growth was caused by a minor baby boom spurred by economic recovery, a measure of stability, and the prospect of a decent, possibly even prosperous long-term future in Trochenbrod.

A rapid expansion of social initiative also started in the mid-1920s and continued into early 1939, with political, spiritual, educational, and cultural expressions. Zionism took strong hold in Trochenbrod, as it did elsewhere in Eastern Europe in this period. Virtually all young people were organized into Zionist movements that spanned the political spectrum from far left to far right. The most robust Zionist youth movement in Trochenbrod was *Beitar*, which had a strong self-defense orientation. Even Ryszard Lubinski, the only Gentile born in Trochenbrod, was close to *Beitar*:

> There were Jewish organizations in Trochenbrod, and sometimes they fought among themselves. Do you know of an organization called *Beitar*? I was close to the people in that organization. The head of it was someone named

Anshel Shpielman. That organization wanted to fight for Palestine, for a Jewish state in Palestine. The other organizations wanted to negotiate for land, and that caused some conflict among them.

The Zionist groups met regularly. Sometimes separately and sometimes in cooperation, they had educational programs; put on plays; held evenings of Hebrew music and dance; conducted special holiday events; promoted the use of modern conversational Hebrew; and sent more than a hundred Jewish "pioneers," to Palestine. A return to the Hebrew language, which was to be the language of the new Jewish state, was one of the basic principles of Zionist youth groups. By the mid-1930s, the language of Trochenbrod, Yiddish, was joined by widespread use of modern Hebrew in homes and at some public meetings. Formal and informal Hebrew language classes proliferated. Trochenbrod, that little isolated town in the midst of Ukrainian villages and forests, even produced poets and essayists who published their work in both Hebrew and Yiddish.

A point of pride among many native Trochenbroders is that in 1938 the first training course outside Palestine for *Etzel* officers was conducted in Trochenbrod. *Etzel* was an early Jewish nationalist organization associated with the *Beitar* Zionist youth movement. *Etzel* members believed in the use of military force to create a Jewish state in Palestine. Menachim Begin, who fought the British in Palestine as a Jewish terrorist and later became prime minister of Israel, was an *Etzel* leader. Trochenbrod offered the nationalist Zionist leaders of *Etzel* a unique set of circumstances for their military training: relative remoteness from the eyes of disapproving Polish authorities; a rural environment with both open land and forest land; a concentration of sympathetic Zionist youth; and a Jewish town that could supply provisions and fraternally accommodate the training.

Alongside the secular Zionist fervor in Trochenbrod, Jewish religious observance, tradition, and scholarship were only slightly diminished there. All the Trochenbroders I spoke with who were young men and women in Trochenbrod in the 1930s had been ardent Zionists, but the men also had been yeshiva students in places like Olyka, Rovno, Mezerich, Lublin, and Warsaw. Many synagogues flourished in Trochenbrod in the mid-1930s—some Trochenbroders told me that as many as nine functioned simultaneously in this small town. Everyone in Trochenbrod followed Orthodox Jewish law and customs. As one Trochenbroder put it, "You were either an Orthodox Jew or they called you a *goy* [Gentile]." Trochenbroders continued to govern their lives and the life of the town by Jewish custom, observe Sabbath prohibitions scrupulously, celebrate all the Jewish holidays robustly as community events, and pray three times each day.

A "Talmud Torah," a Jewish day school for boys that had a number of teachers and taught the classic Jewish religious texts, thrived in Trochenbrod in the mid-1930s, as did many smaller *cheders*. Most children went to Jewish school for a few hours each day after Polish public school. Families that could afford it also hired private teachers for additional Jewish or Hebrew instruction at home.

Trochenbroders who were youngsters in the 1930s reminisce about the Sabbath using the same words as those who experienced Sabbaths in Trochenbrod two or three generations earlier. It was a day for which everyone prepared by baking *chalah* [braided egg bread] and special *chulunt* dishes that would cook all day over a low fire; cleaning themselves and their houses; sending the children door to door collecting baked goods to give to the poor; and dressing in a manner appropriate for greeting and being in the company of "the Sabbath Queen," an affectionate moniker for the special Sabbath day. There were always guests for the Sabbath, often merchants visiting Trochenbrod who could not get home before the start of the holy day, on which travel is forbidden. Everyone who was able happily brought someone home from Friday night prayers to share dinner and their home for the Sabbath.

The women generally left it to their husbands to intercede with God in the synagogue while they, together with their daughters, worked on the special Sabbath meal that was served to the family when the men and boys returned from prayer. Following an after-meal nap, families would go for a stroll, visit relatives, meet in a small park to gossip and talk politics, or perhaps let the children run to find wild blueberries in the Radziwill forest. Sabbath was a day of peace, rest, prayer, family, good eating, socializing, making excursions to the Radziwill forest, singing Sabbath songs and pausing to savor the goodness that God, hard work, and Trochenbrod provided.

Ryszard Lubinski, though he was a Polish Catholic, could not help also being caught up in Trochenbrod's Sabbath:

> There were *Shabbos goys*[3] in Trochenbrod; I helped with that all the time, to light fires for heating and keeping the food warm. We helped our neighbors with that as friends, to keep the fire going. But there were hundreds of houses in Sofiyovka and Ignatovka, so people would come from the villages to tend the fires for the Jews, and made a little money from that. Most of the houses had the same organization: in the kitchen everybody had a stove and an oven to bake bread. I remember that for *Shabbos*, once everything was made, on Friday they would put it inside the bread oven so it would stay warm for the next day. I remember the smell of that very well.

While a bar mitzvah in Trochenbrod was cause for little more than a piece of sponge cake, some fruit, and a taste of schnapps for the men after prayers, weddings were a different matter altogether. Much of the town showed up for the outdoor ceremony. Children recited poems and sang songs, and one of the women baked a huge *challah* and

---

3. "Sabbath Gentile," who performed functions like stoking fires for Jews on the Sabbath because religious law prohibits Jews from doing acts of "work" on that day.

danced while holding it before the bride and groom. It was a time to forget everything else and rejoice. The bride and groom performed their rituals under the wedding canopy— sips of wine, wedding ring, reading of the ritual wedding contract, seven blessings, more sips of wine, and smashing a glass underfoot. A wedding feast was rounded out with schnapps and vodka; a toast, another toast, and then another toast; merry singing and dancing, men with men, to the unbridled exuberance of a klezmer band. A klezmer trio was brought from Kolki for every wedding: Tzalik, who beat the symbols and drums; Chaim, whose fingers danced wildly on the clarinet; and Peshi, the fiddler with a big white beard. There was nothing like a Trochenbrod wedding—that's how it seemed to Trochenbroders.

Under the Polish administration a regional public school was established in Trochenbrod—it was actually located in Shelisht, a hamlet between Trochenbrod and Lozisht that was really a part of Trochenbrod. In this school young Trochenbroders were exposed to Polish-language studies, mathematics, literature, and other secular subjects, and Jewish subjects as well. Ukrainian children from nearby villages also attended this school, and were playmates with their Trochenbrod classmates during the school day. Several Trochenbrod natives to this day have strong memories of participating in Polish-language plays at school, like *Little Red Riding Hood*, even while they rehearsed Yiddish plays in Trochenbrod's cultural center or Hebrew plays in their Zionist groups.

Prince Janush Radziwill—of the same Polish Radziwill family that later in the century Jackie Kennedy's younger sister, Caroline Lee Bouvier, married into—owned vast lands in the region of Trochenbrod. These lands included the forest that bordered fields on the east side of town. The Jews of Trochenbrod often grazed their cattle in the Radziwill forest, took Sabbath walks and picked berries there, from time to time would quietly cut down a tree or two for their own use, and in a manner of speaking considered it *their* forest. This drove a running cat-and-mouse game with Prince Radziwill's forest rangers, but on the whole the people of Trochenbrod had cordial relations with the prince himself. Prince Radziwill's palace was in the small town of Olyka, about twelve miles south of Trochenbrod. To this day there is a horse trail heading south from where Trochenbrod used to be that is known as the Olyka trail.

In the late 1920s, Prince Radziwill built a Catholic church at the edge of his forest, just east of the northern end of Trochenbrod, to serve about thirty Polish families that lived southeast of Trochenbrod. No one knows why he built the church exactly in that place, but the result was that on Sundays a large group of Poles walking to and from church passed through Trochenbrod's muddy street in their go-to-church finery, almost as if promenading in Lutsk, with their priest at the head of the crowd.

Some natives of Trochenbrod recall that young men in these strolling church groups would, as they passed through town, strike at townspeople just to show who was boss.

Tuvia Drori, who was born in Trochenbrod and fled to Palestine in 1939, declared, "Yes, they would hit Jews on their way to church; it was a *mitzvah* [good deed] for them!" But other people who spent their youths in Trochenbrod think the scuffles were incited by young Trochenbrod men who sometimes taunted the Poles on their way to church. Shmulik Potash (not related to Ellie and Basia-Ruchel), who also left for Palestine in 1939, remembers the processions as a good thing for Trochenbrod because while walking through town churchgoers often stopped into Trochenbrod shops to buy things.

Basia-Ruchel Potash was first exposed to serious anti-Jewish behavior by the church processions.

> It was on a Sunday, on the way back from church—they had to pass through our shtetl, the Gentile people—and on the way back from church a bunch of Polish men attacked a bunch of Jewish boys. My uncle was one who was attacked. He was pretty beaten up, black and blue, real real bad. Everyone started to run and close their doors and hide inside because they were afraid for their children and themselves getting beaten up. I saw that with my own eyes. I was screaming, I was hysterical, I was crying. I witnessed other things like that many many times. Mostly it would take place on Sundays, when they would go to or from church through our town. They would call out, "Dirty Jew," or call us names, or hit us. We tried to stay out of their way. It wasn't that bad yet. But through a child's eyes, whatever

I saw had an effect on me: I realized that I'm Jewish and I realized that they don't like us. I realized that I had to be careful and stay out of their way.

Peshia Gotman remembers the church as the object of an adventure more than in connection with the processions:

I remember that church, and how! My mother gave me a good beating because I ran to be at the "otpus"—it's when they have their services outside, it's like a big picnic, it's some kind of ceremony—I was maybe ten years old. I was with a whole bunch of kids. They usually had ice cream, and all kinds of toys; it was like a big picnic, the whole church was having a picnic outside. I got a big spanking for that, because I was not supposed to go to the church.

Perhaps Prince Radziwill had devious intent when he set things up so that Trochenbroders would be drawn to their windows and yards by weekly church processions and would have a relatively good view of the church and the goings-on in its yard. While there were many different perspectives on the subject, there's no escaping the fact that in the 1930s, the Polish Catholic church and the weekly churchgoer processions were prominent in the life of the Jewish town of Trochenbrod.

By the mid-1930s, many Trochenbroders who had emigrated before World War I, particularly to the United States, managed, despite the Depression, to return to Trochenbrod to visit the town and their relatives. David Shwartz was one of those people. His memoir was inspired by a visit he paid to Trochenbrod with his wife in 1934. Basia-Ruchel Potash remembers with great clarity even today a visit by American relatives well over seventy-five years ago:

> In 1933 an aunt and uncle of ours came to visit us. Of course we had a big open house, all of Trochenbrod was invited, and everybody came to the party to honor my aunt from America who had been sixteen or seventeen years old when she left for the United States. They were like big celebrities today. It was so much fun. I was asking her stories about America. I was so curious; I remember her telling us about black people in America, and I couldn't understand what she was talking about. At the party we took a picture of everyone; and what do you think happened in the middle of taking a picture? The cow came and left some droppings. Everybody laughed; that was funny—in our backyard.

Those who visited reported mixed stories. Most remembered their Trochenbrod with fondness and a rich sense of community and Jewish life that was missing for them in America, and felt freshly the pangs of longing for that way of life when they visited. But they were Americans now, and many saw Trochenbrod's relative prosperity through American eyes as unacceptable poverty, primitiveness, and removal from modern urban living. Visitors from abroad often brought with them envelopes of dollars, some for their own relatives and some for relatives of their Trochenbrod friends in the States. Eastern European Jewish immigrants in the United States were getting increasingly nervous about Hitler's rise, and many of the visitors came to Trochenbrod with the aim of convincing relatives to leave. One family tells of their grandparents going back carrying extra suitcases for the Trochenbrod family members they had hoped they could persuade to leave.

Despite being the only Jewish town in Europe, Trochenbrod was never widely known, even among Jews. But its unique character meant that neither was it quite as obscure as thousands of other Eastern European *shtetls*. More than a few Jews sought it out as a place to live and many more as a place to visit, a place where they could see and breathe the air of a Jewish town—and good country air, at that. The special quality of Jewish life in Trochenbrod may have contributed to creating a somewhat outsized share of relative notables in the Jewish world. Eliezer Burak, a Trochenbroder who moved to Palestine as a Jewish pioneer in the 1920s, wrote an article about his beloved Trochenbrod that was published in Hebrew in Tel Aviv in 1945. In it he recalls a handful of Trochenbrod's "famous people" from just before and during the interwar period, especially those who helped spread Jewish culture.

> Rabbi Yehezkel Potash, the permanent "Starusta" [gov-
> ernment-appointed "Elder"] of the town in the days of
> the Czarist government. He was a scholarly and learned

man, and served the people of Trochenbrod well with his honesty and intelligence.

Hirsch Kantor, a comedian who was master of his profession and very talented. At weddings and other gatherings he would bring joy to everyone with his rhymes and his cleverness.

Rabbi Moshe Hirsch Roitenberg, the scholar, ran a cheder in the town, and also served as a cantor, and he too had great talent as a comedian. His jokes were published in the newspapers *Heint* and *Moment*, which pleased him a great deal. Journalists would come all the way from Warsaw to interview him.

Two high-level Communists: Motel Shwartz who was a well-known Commissar in the Odessa fleet, and Yaakov Burak who was an admiral on a Russian warship and a university graduate. In the period of the Soviet purges Shwartz disappeared, and Burak drowned with his ship near Kronstadt in the war between the Bolsheviks and the Whites. These two had studied many years in the Slobodka yeshiva, and Motel Shwartz was even a certified rabbi.

Yisrael Beider, a son of the Rabbi Moshe David Beider, was a teacher in nearby Olyka, and after that moved to Mezerich near Brisk [Brest-Litovsk] and continued his literary work as a poet and essayist in both Hebrew and Yiddish.

Yitzhak Aronski, a young and talented journalist, a feature writer published widely in Polish Jewish newspapers. He helped establish "The Volyner Shtima," which

was published in Rovno, and founded a library in Trochenbrod as part of his personal mission to encourage
widespread reading of newspapers and books.

Hitler goose-stepped onto the scene in Europe, became
chancellor of Germany in 1933, and in 1934 signed the
German-Polish nonaggression pact. Among other things, the
pact essentially left no restrictions on Nazi propaganda in
Poland. From 1934 until Hitler's invasion of western Poland
in 1939, Poland's repression of Jews, along with anti-Jewish
hooliganism and actual pogroms, echoed those in Germany
with slightly less shrillness. Relatives abroad were urging
Trochenbrod families to leave. But Trochenbrod had not
been directly affected much by anti-Jewish hooliganism,
apart from the occasional Sunday brawl, and was prospering
and modernizing like never before. The few who did con-
sider leaving were torn.

By the late 1930s, Trochenbrod had become *the* place to
shop and do business in the region. Many elderly Ukrainians today remember visiting Trochenbrod as children
with their parents, and being awestruck at everything that
was available for sale there, at the nice houses ("like ours, but
bigger, better, nicer, and with nice things in them"), and at the
hustle and bustle in the street. The intense regional commercial activity in Trochenbrod meant that during the workday,
parts of the town were a Babel of Ukrainian, Polish, Yiddish,
Hebrew, German, and sometimes Russian—and when relatives visited from the United States, English too. The commer-

cial hubbub during the workday was such that one almost forgot that this was a Jewish town.

One elderly woman in Horodiche, a Ukranian village about four miles southeast of Trochenbrod through the forest, told me that as a child she would beg her father to take her with him on his shopping excursions to Sofiyovka because for her it was like going to the big city. A Ukrainian from the village of Yaromel about two miles away remembered "beautiful stores there, lots of different kinds of stores." He also remembered Trochenbrod shopkeepers as gentle and kind people:

> We bought things there: fabrics, clothes, shoes, and other things. If we needed to buy something but we didn't have the money, the Jewish shopkeepers would say, "Don't worry, it's OK; when you'll have the money, you'll pay me." They were good people. They trusted everyone.

An old-timer from the nearby village of Domashiv reminisced:

> They hired Ukrainians from nearby villages to work in their fields. Ukrainians from the surrounding villages would go there to try to find something to do to earn money. They could get two zlotys for helping in the fields, and the Trochenbroders would give them a cup of tea. They would even hire Ukrainians to cut their grasses for their cattle because the Trochenbrod people were

busy trading. They were selling all sorts of leather goods, and they were buying animals for hides to make leather to make those goods.

Before the war everyone was friendly. The Jews, Ukrainians, and Poles all had different professions and did business with each other. People from different villages went around to other villages. They might sew clothes, or repair something in someone's house. Everyone had his own job, so it was peaceful and friendly, and everyone had his own piece of land and worked on it.

A woman in a formerly Polish village, Przebradze, on what used to be the principal road from Trochenbrod to Kivertzy and Lutsk, knew Trochenbrod and many of its people well:

> My parents used to take me to Sofiyovka because there were a lot of shops there where we could by a lot of things. The people from all the villages around Sofiyovka went there to get everything they needed.
>
> We had bees, and we sold honey there in the summer. We took the honey there by horse wagon. People came with jars or whatever containers they had, and my grandfather poured the honey into it. We brought the honey in a bucket, and strawberries also, to sell along the street.

In the final years of the 1930s, modern technology began to find its way to Trochenbrod. The first electricity, radios, bicycles, even movies—Basia-Ruchel Potash remembers one of the 1930s *Gold Diggers* series—made their appearances. The Yiddish newspaper *Forward* was delivered regularly. The district administration office in the village of Silno, not far from Horodiche, acquired an automobile that enabled local officials to visit villages and towns in the district when the dirt roads were passable. Trochenbrod's post office now also offered telephone and telegraph service. Improved (but not paved) roads made travel to the train station at Kivertzy and to Lutsk routine, though it was still problematic after a rain.

November 10, 1938: Kristallnacht. Most of Trochenbrod's more than five thousand Jews could not imagine that Hitler's storm was really as bad as people said—or in any case that it would blow on their pleasant, friendly, and industrious town whose people served everyone in the region well and caused trouble to no one.

Because Trochenbrod was a consequential regional trading and production center, the district administration planted more trees; installed bollards to keep traffic out of the drainage ditches along Trochenbrod's only street; and even began to upgrade the street, which often became muddy and impassable for wagons, with paving stones—a sort of downtown renewal project. The project to pave Trochenbrod's street was begun in 1938. Peshia Gotman watched the paving work as a seventeen-year-old preparing to immigrate to the United States. Though she did leave, she recalls desperately not wanting to.

To me Trochenbrod looked like a street that had been

picked up from a city and plopped down somewhere in the wilderness, except that the street was mud. Seeing the street being paved convinced me that what we all expected was starting to happen—Trochenbrod was going to become a city, a Jewish city. Why would I leave it?

The ribbon-cutting for the first small paved section of Trochenbrod's street was held in the spring of 1939. That was the last section paved.

On August 23, 1939, Germany and the U.S.S.R. signed the Molotov-Ribbentrop nonaggression pact. On September 1, Germany invaded Poland from the west, and two weeks later the Soviet Union invaded Poland from the east, taking territory it had failed to keep in its war with Poland twenty years earlier. Trochenbrod came under Soviet rule once again. The Second World War had begun.

At that moment everything began to change. So this is a good time to let Shmulik Potash remind us what the essence of Trochenbrod was before dusk:

> Although there were plenty of poor people in Trochenbrod, they were all wealthy. Why? Because they felt their lives were rich and they were satisfied. There's a saying, "Want what you have, and then you'll have what you want." Ninety-five percent of Trochenbrod people were like that. They were salt of the earth, as they say. The very concept of stealing was unknown to them—take something that belongs to someone else, what's that?

The people who read your book, I want to tell them that there once was a Jewish town of worthy people, hard-working people, honest people, trusting people. All they wanted was to raise children who would also be good people. That's what Trochenbrod was.

OPPOSITE: *Between the wars. A paved road runs from the city of Lutsk, in the lower left corner, about 8 miles northeast to the Kivertzy railroad station. From there the road continues unpaved about 20 miles northeast to the much smaller city of Kolki. Following that road from the Kivertzy railroad station, just past the village of Ozero you would have turned right to Przebradze on your way to Trochenbrod. Passing by the entrance to Kol. Yosefin on the left, you would have entered Trochenbrod from the south. To Trochenbrod's southeast is Horodiche. Silno, the administrative center, is slightly northeast of that. In the southeast corner of the map is the town of Olyka. Northeast of Trochenbrod is Klubochin, a village from which Ukrainian partisans cooperated with those from Trochenbrod during the German occupation. Northeast of Klubochin is Lopaten, where Medvedev had his partisan headquarters. Immediately northwest of Trochenbrod is its sister village of Lozisht. Just northwest of Lozisht is the village of Domashiv, and southwest of that is the village of Yaromel. Due west of Domashiv is Trostjanets, where you would turn left to get to Trochenbrod-Lozisht if you were coming from Kolki. The paved road eastward from Lutsk connects it to the city of Rovno.*

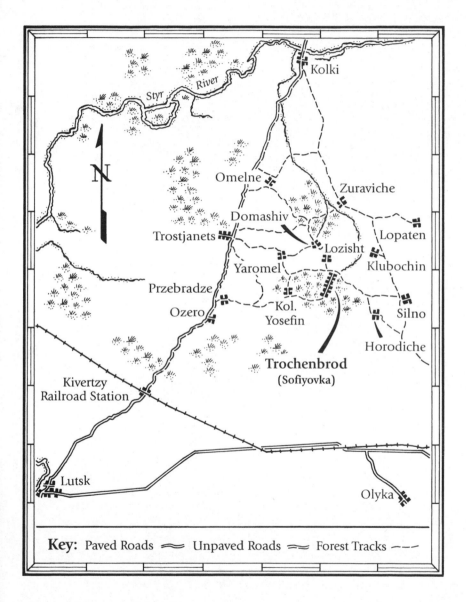

Chapter Three

DUSK

In October 1939, Trochenbrod came under Soviet rule once again. But this time there was a well-organized cell of Communists in Trochenbrod to greet and work with Soviet officials. Trochenbrod Communists had been underground during Polish rule, and now they were joined by Communist comrades, both Jewish and Gentile, freed by the Soviets from Polish prisons. The transition to Communist ways started immediately.

—

For this brief era in Trochenbrod's history, I was able to gather most of the information from living people. By and large, these people had remarkable stories to tell and observations to make—as one might expect of people who escaped or survived the Holocaust. Their first-person accounts are treasures for the way they express what happened in Trochenbrod and how it felt during its darkening last days.

Local Jewish Communists were installed as mayor, police, and other local officials in Trochenbrod. The Polish post office was closed. The Soviets took over much of the economic property in Trochenbrod—small factories, workshops, even some shops. Typically they put the workers, whether one or a half dozen, in charge, and turned the owner into a worker. Most family enterprises without workers were allowed to continue, but a few were taken over "for the people" by upper-level Communists. People were being driven into poverty, and at the same time, shortages were developing. Food was rationed through a cooperative store. People hid property, including their stocks of food, and a black market for basic necessities developed. The town was pushed steadily in the direction of people having little money, but in any case, there was little to buy.

The Soviets were not particularly anti-Jewish, and when they took over the public school they allowed the language of instruction for Trochenbrod pupils to be Yiddish, though of course all students also had to study Russian. Consistent with Communist ideology, the Soviets strongly discouraged religious observance—they interfered with synagogue prayers and tried to impose labor on the Sabbath. But in the end, because on a day-to-day basis things were run mostly by local people, ways could often be found to circumvent Communist doctrine. The flavor of this is captured in the memories of Tuvia Drori as he told them to me and also as he wrote about them in his book *Ani Ma'amin* (*I Believe*):

> Everybody knew everybody in our small town. Together we played, and as we grew up we talked and argued. We *Beitar* people knew the secrets of the Communist underground (and sometimes we helped them against the Polish police), and they were aware of our *Etzel* courses held in town (the last one was at the beginning of 1939). They knew we had weapons and that we were using live ammunition during the drills because they heard the gunshots.
>
> When the Soviets arrived in October 1939, at first they tried to pull us into Communist activity and convince us to become Communists, which would also be good for our work and social situations; they tried to draw us to their assemblies, social activities, and theatrical shows, but we did not oblige.
>
> Then they decided (probably because of pressures from above) to arrest us. In my case it was one of my former pupils who came to arrest me. In the first interrogation we were asked about the weapons we had and

whether the *Beitar* youth organization was still active. We didn't take those interrogations too seriously. The social closeness among us was too strong for them to do us any harm.

Eventually we were released and returned home, but it was obvious we could not sit idly waiting for the next arrest. The hopes that maybe the war would cease and we would be able to continue our Zionist activities were diminishing. Contacts with the outside world were cut off completely, and we could not bear staying citizens under Stalin's regime.

At the end of autumn a group of us from *Beitar* decided to start moving out, to find a way to *Eretz Yisrael* [the Land of Israel]. We knew we would have to steal borders, and who knew where we would end up, as we would be going only on uncharted routes.

Soon after arrival of the Soviets, between twenty and thirty Trochenbrod young people, like Tuvia and his *Beitar* friends, began sneaking away with the aim of finding a path to Palestine. They usually left at night and suffered tearful and tragic separations from their families, or slipped out without a face-to-face good-bye because their parents did not want them to leave. None of them ever saw their families again.

Most made their way to Vilna (Vilnius), where a shelter, the "Internat," had been established for young people who were fleeing to Palestine from all over Eastern Europe. From

Vilna there were many ways these young people made their ways to Palestine, traveling through Turkey, Russia, Kazakhstan, Uzbekistan, Afghanistan, Iran, Iraq, Syria, Egypt, Transjordan, and more. Travel through Europe was no longer safe. It took most of them one or two years to make the trip; it took many much longer. Quite a few fell out of contact during their journeys and were never heard from again. A few got stuck along the way in Moscow and ended up fading into Soviet society.

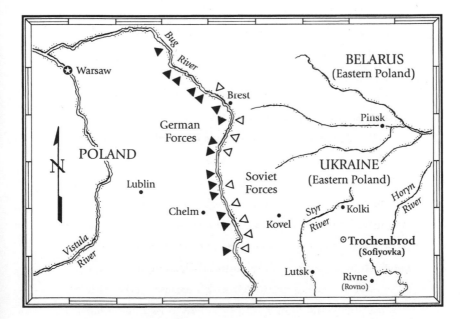

Soviet–German Line, 1940

Here is Hanna Tziporen's story: she was eighteen years old
when she left Trochenbrod in 1939.

I was in *Beitar*, and there was a leader there named
Anshel Shpielman. When the war broke out and the
Soviets came in we knew there was no way but to try
to escape to *Eretz Yisrael*, to Palestine. When Anshel
explored if there was some way we could get there,
we heard that if we could find a way to get to Vilna
in Lithuania it might be possible to go from there to
Palestine. Getting to Vilna was not so easy either, but
let's not dwell on that.

I went with a friend of mine, Machli Schuster. After
we arrived in Vilna, we slept together in one bed;
there was only one toilet for everyone; one shower for
everyone; we had a communal kitchen. There were Jews
there who gave work to refugees like us, so that we'd be
able to earn some money.

In Vilna there were a number of people from Trochenbrod, and many others, trying to get to Palestine.
We had to find a place to go where we could earn some
money. A rich Jew named Goldberg owned a commercial farm in Mergaloukus, not too far from Kovno
(Kaunus), and he let us go there. The men worked in the
fields, in tobacco, and the women helped in the house.

We wanted to get to Moscow, because we heard it
was possible to go onward from there to Palestine. One
day we were notified that there was a way now to do

this. A fellow named Avram, from Pinsk, came to help us for the journey. We needed money for the journey and the visas. Someone was sent to Lutsk, and somehow got the $100 from our parents to get us to Moscow and then maybe a little bit further.

In Moscow people went to the Turkish consulate to request transit permits to Palestine. But at that time there were so many refugees that the British asked the Turks to refuse the laissez-passer requests so that there would not be so many Jews coming into Palestine. We wandered around Moscow not knowing what to do. A Jew there recommended that we go to the Persian embassy. So I went, together with people from all sorts of political parties, not just *Beitar*. I received a false entry permit for Iran. A group of more than thirty of us got to Iran.

We stayed in Teheran several months. Then we were told we had to leave Teheran, so we went to the city of Meshet. There we waited: what will become of us, how will we get to *Eretz Yisrael*? At that time Iran was having a war with Iraq, so Iraq wouldn't let us pass. So we went through the desert by train, and made our way to Suez. While on the train we learned that the Soviet-German war had broken out—that the Germans had invaded eastern Poland, where Trochenbrod was, that had been in Soviet hands.

We went through the Suez Canal by cargo boat, and arrived at Haifa. There the British arrested us and jailed us. We were in the jail for a couple of months, and then

the British freed us. They couldn't send us back to anywhere, and that's how we arrived in *Eretz Yisrael*.

Shmulik Potash has a different sort of story to tell. He
left Trochenbrod in 1939 to work at a training farm near
Lodz, Poland, run by the General Zionist organization.
Jewish youngsters went to this place from everywhere in
Eastern Europe to prepare themselves, by learning farming
skills, to live in a Jewish farming settlement in Palestine.
When the Germans invaded Poland, Shmulik quickly
decided to return to Trochenbrod by way of Warsaw to say
good-bye to family and friends and then make his way to
Palestine.

A couple of days after he got to Warsaw the city was surrounded and besieged by the German army. The Germans
rained artillery shells and bombs on the city for three weeks,
and effectively leveled about a third of it. Shmulik was stuck
there. He knew no one in Warsaw. He wandered around
with the bombing going on around him, and by some
miracle survived. Then, as he tells it, on the eve of the Jewish
holiday of *Sukkot* the Germans conquered Warsaw. Massed
German troops were waiting at the edge of the city to swarm
in and occupy it.

By climbing across the rubble of a bridge on the Vistula
River, Shmulik escaped to a relatively rural eastern suburb of
Warsaw called Praga. German troops were there, but having
conquered Warsaw—in fact, all of western Poland—they
were relaxed about letting people move around a bit. For

three days Shmulik wandered around Praga trying to figure out what to do. He had nothing to eat. At one point he had an encounter with a German soldier, with whom he communicated coarsely on the basis of his Yiddish. The soldier, a young man about nineteen years old, challenged Shmulik's presence in an old tomato field. Shmulik had been rooting around in the soil looking for scraps to eat. In the end the soldier made a sausage sandwich from food he had in his knapsack, gave it to Shmulik, and then warned him away because there were mines in the field.

The next day the Germans opened the concertina wire they had strung around the city, and as the German soldiers flooded in, people fleeing eastward were able to slip out, Shmulik among them.

He moved eastward on foot and hitching rides in passing horse-drawn wagons, and describes with wonderment his second positive experience with a German soldier:

We were walking along the road, and a horse-drawn wagon passed with two German soldiers, one driving it. I raised my arm, they came up to me, and the driver said, "Sure, hop on." The two soldiers were talking—I couldn't hear what they were saying because of the noise of the wheels. Suddenly, the one who was not driving turns and looks at me, and jerks his head toward the side of the road in a signal that I should jump off the wagon; the one who was holding the reins didn't see that he did this. I understood his signal and jumped. The driver was

probably talking about robbing or beating me. A second
German soldier had helped me survive.

The Soviets had established a very strong border guard—
cavalry, foot soldiers, jeep-mounted troops, guards with
dogs—because they were worried about infiltration by
German spies. After several failed attempts over several days
to steal the border, Shmulik threw caution to the wind one
night, sprinted as fast as he could when he saw an opening,
and made it, much to his own surprise. A few days later he
was back in Trochenbrod where his arrival was greeted with
a joyous celebration. He found Communists in charge.

Word soon reached Trochenbrod about the way station to
Palestine that had been set up in Vilna, and Shmulik made
his way there. There were no serious border issues because
the Soviets were now in control all the way north through
Lithuania. From Vilna he went to Moscow. Moscow was
followed by a long string of twists and turns that landed
Shmulik in one strange place, like Tashkent, after another. It
was ten years later, in 1949, that Shmulik finally arrived in
what by then had become the State of Israel.

During this period of Soviet control, despite the
changes—growing poverty, loss of businesses, pressure
to join the Communist Party or Communist youth organizations, pressure to abandon Judaism, constantly being
watched and worrying about being reported for something, frequent interrogations—the people of Trochenbrod
could still move about relatively freely, and to some degree

maintain their way of life. Meanwhile, many Jews from western Poland fled the Nazis into Soviet-held territory, and about a thousand of them found their way to Trochenbrod and Lozisht.

The story that Nahum Kohn tells in his book, *A Voice from the Forest: Memoirs of a Jewish Partisan*, conveys a good sense of what it was like in and around Trochenbrod in those times. Nahum was born and raised in western Poland. Soon after the German invasion he fled eastward and found himself in Lutsk. In Lutsk he eventually found his brother, a friend from his hometown, and the friend's older brother, all of whom had also fled to what had been eastern Poland, now controlled by the Soviets.

Nahum was a trained and experienced watchmaker. He found work for several months with another watchmaker that he had come across who had a little business in Lutsk. Under Soviet rules, a person could work on his own but could not have employees. By early 1940 the Soviets had organized their administration sufficiently to fully enforce their idea of socialism, and Nahum had to go to work for a state-run collective for watchmakers. One day, after many months, Soviet officials rounded up the refugees from western Poland in Lutsk and sent them on their way to Siberia, probably concerned that there were spies for Germany among them. Soon after the train was under way, Nahum and a few others jumped off. The escapees included Nahum's hometown friend and his older brother and a new friend who was also a watchmaker. They hid in a forest—probably the Radziwill forest—for a few days and then Nahum and his friends walked back to Lutsk.

They found their way to a large livery stable, where they hid with the help of the Jewish owner. They needed to work and earn money, so after a week of hiding Nahum took a chance and went to the local Soviet government office and asked how he could find work. After looking at Nahum's documents the official understood that Nahum was not supposed to be there, but he was sympathetic. He conspicuously pretended everything was in order and told Nahum that he was not allowed to work in Lutsk but could find work in a small lumbering town twenty-five miles to the east. When Nahum reported this back at the livery stable they all understood that the idea was simply to get away from Lutsk, and the stable owner had a better idea for that.

He told them that not far from Lutsk there were "two villages of Jewish peasants." A friend of his from there by the name of Schuster would visit him soon, and he would see if "something can be arranged." It turned out that something could indeed be arranged, and soon Nahum and his friends were looking, wide-eyed, down the street of a now much poorer Trochenbrod.

> When we arrived there, it was the first time in my life that I saw Jewish farmers. I could never have imagined this, and I rejoiced when I saw them. Everyone had primitive leather-working equipment at home, and they worked on hides. So they lived from their fields, their

cows, their horses, and their hides. They were totally surrounded by forests; the nearest road was twenty or thirty kilometers away. I was curious, so I used to ask old-timers how they came to be there. They told me that the area had been totally unsettled and wild when their ancestors came . . .

With our watch-repairing skills we could earn something. The people in Trochenbrod-Ignatovka didn't have wristwatches, but they had ancient clocks on their walls, and before our arrival there had been no watchmaker. So they brought these antiques to us and bartered food in exchange for repairs . . .

A number of months after Nahum's arrival in Trochenbrod the German army invaded and took control. Nahum soon went into the forest and put together a small partisan group mostly of Trochenbroders. They dedicated themselves to disrupting German army units and supply trains and taking revenge on Ukrainians who betrayed their neighbors and had tortured and murdered Jews or turned them over to the Germans. The unit was eventually decimated by the Germans and their collaborators. Nahum and two other survivors found and joined a Soviet partisan detachment led by a famous partisan commander, Dmitry Medvedev, headquartered in the Lopaten forest a few miles northeast of Trochenbrod.

Basia-Ruchel Potash had what she remembers as a rich and wonderful childhood in Trochenbrod, despite her brushes with small-time anti-Jewish hooliganism among the Sunday churchgoers. That started to change as soon as the Soviets took control. You can hear in her brief childhood memories of that period a steadily rising tension as Soviet control unfolds toward a Nazi takeover.

I remember in 1939 the Russians came and took over our *shtetl*. They made us go to the Russian school, and they wanted us all to join their youth organization—they gave us little scarves and called us "Young Pioneers."

They told us all to report anybody who said things against the Russians. But the influence of our parents at home overrode anything they told us. We knew we had to be quiet, not to say certain things, behave in a certain way. They would send you to Siberia if you made a wrong move. And then you had the left-wingers, a few of them; they could turn you in too. Those Socialists, they were so excited, they thought the Russians would take away from us and give it to them. It didn't work that way. The Russians kept the businesses and made those people managers or whatever, but they didn't share with them the wealth of the others. Some of them followed the Russians when they left. They followed them to Russia.

When the war with Germany broke out in 1941, they were going to take my father into the Red Army. My father didn't want to go to the army. So we had a secret, my dad and I. There was a certain flower, dandelions I think, and he told me that I should go out and pick these flowers, and we would go above, in the attic in our house, and he rubbed the flower on his arm, and he'd wrap it around, and eventually it caused tremendous sores on his arm, really bad—I think they would amputate it here in America. He did it to stay out of the army. I'm the only one who knew about it: not my brothers, nobody. When his arm was ripe and ready at last, that's just when the Russians left and the Germans, Hitler, took over.

I remember the first thing was that planes flew over and the bombs were dropping. They came out of nowhere, and people started running into the woods. The Radziwill forest was right in back of our *shtetl* so people began running there, or hiding in their gardens, or lying down wherever they could. I don't know how many bombs were dropping, but I never heard anything like this, the sounds of the bombs, and screams and hysterics of the mothers and the babies and children. I was hiding next door in the garden, and I saw a bomb drop and kill my brother's goat. It destroyed our garden and a few homes, and some people were injured. They were flying very very low, just on top of the roofs. We could see the soldiers, the Nazis, inside the plane when we looked up, that's how low they were flying. It was devastating. What did they bomb for? Obviously they just wanted to kill civilians because there was nothing to bomb in Trochenbrod, just the houses.

In accordance with the terms of its nonaggression pact with Germany, the Kremlin muted the Soviet press about

Nazi treatment of Jewish people. While some information arrived with refugees who fled east from Poland, and some radio reports filtered in, the people of Trochenbrod suffered a combination of ignorance and denial about the magnitude of what was happening to Jews under the Nazis. This ignorance and denial kept some from fleeing with the Soviets when Germany invaded. Even after Germany invaded, many Trochenbroders remembered the milder treatment at the hands of "Germans" than at the hands of Russians in World War I and simply did not—could not—believe that the Germans would treat them as terribly as some were saying.

Trochenbrod and its sister village of Lozisht had a combined population of over six thousand Jewish souls when the Germans invaded Soviet-held lands on June 22, 1941. In the first days after their invasion of Trochenbrod the Germans marked the town's houses with Jewish stars, carried out random murders, and invited destruction and looting of Jewish possessions by rampaging Ukrainian villagers freed from restraint by the departure of the Soviets. The Germans immediately set up a local administration system. This included a Judenrat, or Jewish Council, to help carry out German orders like providing Jews for forced labor or collecting "taxes" for the Germans. The German administration system also included Ukrainian auxiliary police and a Ukrainian militia to do the work of policing the Jews, hunting them down when they tried to escape the terror, and assisting the liquidations.

The auxiliary police were known as Schutsmen (*Schutz* is the German word for protection); many of them saw their new roles as nothing more than opportunities for looting, extortion, and brutalizing Jews. The militia tended to be made up of members of the Organization of Ukrainian Nationalists (OUN). Known as "Banderovtsi," after their ultranationalist leader Stepan Bandera, they were virulently anti-Jewish, and vicious. They worked closely with the Germans as a convenience: their aim was to purify Ukraine by ridding it of Jews, Poles, Russians, and ultimately Germans, and fulfill the long-cherished dream of an independent and "pure" Ukraine. People with whom Trochenbroders had friendly relations before, people from nearby villages, suddenly turned up as collaborators with the Nazi regime and treated their Trochenbrod neighbors with cruelty and brutality.

The Germans wasted no time establishing terror and death as the distinguishing marks of their occupation, particularly for Jews. At the beginning of July they had their Schutsmen gather 150 Trochenbrod men, men selected by the Judenrat, and ship them by truck to Kivertzy. Everyone understood, or perhaps just assumed, that this was a work crew for the railroad depot. At Kivertzy the men were handed over to a detachment of German soldiers, who took them to the yard of the local jailhouse and slaughtered them. Word of what happened came back to Trochenbrod immediately.

Like other settlements, Trochenbrod had to supply a quota of laborers who were sent mostly to Kivertzy to work for the Germans. The Judenrat had to make arrangements to meet the quota, but the Schutsmen would also snatch people off the street for these work crews. Each work crew labored a week or so before it was replaced by the next. The workers slept on the floors in empty warehouses and stables near the railroad station. They worked mostly loading and unloading trains but were put to other heavy work for the Germans as well, like digging trenches or hauling building supplies or doing construction work. At night the men in these crews would be beaten and terrorized by their Ukrainian guards and German overseers; some men never returned.

In October, Trochenbrod's agricultural farmsteads were confiscated, as were the townspeople's furs, other warm clothing, and valuable property like farm equipment. The Jews were also commanded to pay a heavy burden of special taxes. Meanwhile, Schutsmen and Banderovtsi extorted gold, silver, and other valuables from them. Jewish life in Trochenbrod became worthless. The temptation and opportunity this provided to walk into the homes of their Jewish neighbors and take what they wanted was, for some Ukrainians, irresistible.

Soon after, the Germans ordered that all Trochenbrod's cattle be brought to the Kivertzy train station for shipment to Germany. Schutsmen on horses gleefully rounded up the cattle and shipped them off. This basically ended any means for most Jews to support themselves. They were not allowed to leave the town, work the fields, or trade with people outside the town. Again a black market developed, this time more extensive and also more risky than under the

TOP: Trochenbrod today, looking south. BOTTOM: Spot near the site of Trochenbrod where tractors and horse carts ford the creek even today. This could be Trochim Ford, but there is no way to know for certain. *Photos by the author.*

Mennonitische Siedlungen
im westukrainischen Raume
1:2 000 000

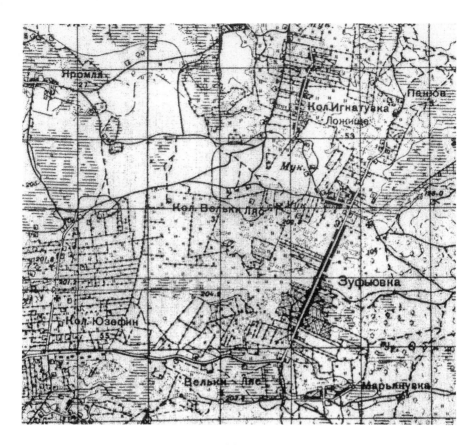

OPPOSITE TOP: A field near the site of Trochenbrod today. The reeds mark a creek. Though the area is now drained, this photo hints of what the first settlers at Trochim Ford found at the site. *Photo by the author.* OPPOSITE BOTTOM: Segment of a map of Mennonite settlements in western Ukraine in the 1800s, from the Mennonite Historical Atlas, 1996. The original Mennonite village of Sofiyovka (Zofijowka) on the Horyn River is in the upper right corner. The newer settlements of Yosefin (Jozefin) and Sofiyovka (Zofjowka) are to the southwest, between the Horyn and Styr Rivers, northeast of Lutsk (Luck). Map provided by Helmut T. Huebert, principal author of the Mennonite Historical Atlas. ABOVE: Russian map, 1890. Trochenbrod's name is given only as "Zufiyuvka." The town, with its distinctive one long street and larger size than other settlements in the area, is prominent in the southeast quadrant of the map. Its sister village to the northwest, "Kol. Ignatuvka" has the additional name "Lozhishe" under it, though it was actually known as "Lozisht." In the southwest quadrant is "Kol. Yuzefin," originally established by Mennonites and later peopled by "Volksdeutch."

3

TOP: Stylized sketch of Trochenbrod adapted from the back cover of the book, Hailan V'shoreshav (*The Tree and Its Roots: The History of T.L., Sofiyovka-Ignatovka*), the Trochenbrod-Lozisht memorial book. The image appears here courtesy of the Israeli Bet-Tal organization, an organization formally established in the 1950s to preserve the memory of the people of Trochenbrod and Lozisht. BOTTOM LEFT: Glass production remnant recovered by the author from the site of the glass factory in Trochenbrod. A principal product of the factory was medicine bottles, which accounts for the green tint. BOTTOM RIGHT: Candlestick from Trochenbrod, likely from well before World War I. Probably part of a pair for a Friday evening ritual used to welcome the Sabbath day. Presented as a gift to the author by Ivan Podziubanchuk.

TOP: Matzah cover for the Passover *seder* [ritual meal], made in Trochenbrod in 1913 by Elke Antwarg as part of her wedding trousseau. Provided by granddaughter Miriam Antwarg Ciocler. BOTTOM LEFT: Wall clock crafted in Trochenbrod in 1914 by Michael Antwarg. The clockwork came from Switzerland. Several generations of Antwargs were carpenters and woodworkers. *Photo by granddaughter Miriam Antwarg Ciocler*. BOTTOM RIGHT: Bullet from World War I that was embedded in a tree near Trochenbrod. Presented as a gift to the author by Ivan Podziubanchuk.

TOP: Engagement photo of Elke and Michael Antwarg, Trochenbrod, 1913. The photo was probably made in a studio in Lutsk. The couple and their children immigrated to Brazil in 1933. *Photo provided by granddaughter Miriam Antwarg Ciocler.*
BOTTOM: Late 1800s portrait of a Trochenbrod couple, family name Cohen. Appears to be a retouched studio photograph. *Photo provided by great-great-granddaughter Laura Beeler.*

Portrait photograph of Idah-Sarah and Isaac Weiner and two of their daughters in Trochenbrod in the late 1800s or early twentieth century. Backdrop appears to be set up in someone's house or a public building. Their son immigrated to the United States in 1906; the rest of the family remained in Trochenbrod. *Photo provided by great-granddaughter Miriam Weiner Bernhardt.*

Sofiyovka birth records, 1918. Left side in Polish, right side in Hebrew. Signed by B. Rojtenberg (Duv Ber Rojtenberg), who was the Cazone Rabbi—the official government-appointed rabbi who kept certain civil records. This book was found in the State Archive of Volyn Region, in Lutsk. *Photo by the author.*

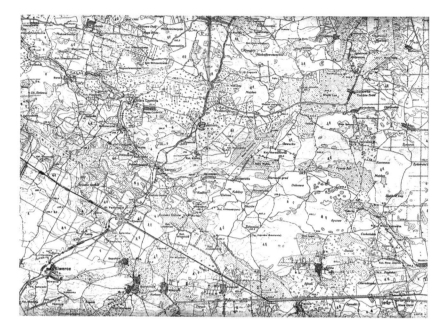

Polish map, 1933. Lutsk is just off the lower left corner of the map. The road from Lutsk to Kolki runs northeast through Kivertzy (Kiwerce), crosses the railroad tracks at Kivertzy station, passes by the village of Jezioro (Ozero) built around a lake (notice symbols for both a church and synagogue there), and here is shown continuing on as far as a village of houses lining a horizontal street in the top center of the map. The village, name not shown, is Trostjanets, located about halfway between Kivertzy station and Kolki. Normally, coming to Trochenbrod from Lutsk, Kivertzy, or the train station, you'd turn right just beyond Jezioro, on the road that passes through Przebrodz (Przebradze), and continue east to the southern end of Trochenbrod. Coming from Kolki southward, you'd turn left at Trostjanets and pass through Yaromel (Jaromla) or Domashiv (Domaszow) and approach Trochenbrod from the northern end. The Domashiv route would bring you through Trochenbrod's sister "colony" of Ignatovka (Kol. Ignatowka), also called Lozisht (Lozyszcze). Note Trochenbrod's size relative to other settlements in the region.

ABOVE: Polish map, 1933. Larger-scale view of Trochenbrod and the surrounding settlements, including Horodiche (Horodysze), at the lower right. Notice the symbol for a church, Radziwill's church, a bit east of the triangular intersection at the northern end of Trochenbrod. Villagers from Klubochin (Klobuczyn), at the upper right, worked closely with Trochenbrod partisans during World War II. OPPOSITE TOP: Trochenbroders photographed in 1930 by Ruchel Abrams, while on a visit from Cleveland, Ohio. *Photo provided by Burton and Ellen Singerman.* OPPOSITE BOTTOM: Rabbi Moshe Hirsch Roitenberg, a widely recognized scholar and something of a Trochenbrod celebrity. Photo dated in the mid 1930s. It was copied from the book, *Hailan V'shoreshav (The Tree and Its Roots: The History of T.L., Sofiyovka-Ignatovka)*, the Trochenbrod-Lozisht memorial book, and appears here courtesy of the Israeli Bet-Tal organization.

TOP: Trochenbrod's post office, late 1930s. Originally built as a house, a section of the roof (above the postman, standing) could be opened to the sky for the *Sukkot* holiday, the Feast of Tabernacles. Polish postmistress Janina Lubinski is standing in the doorway. She hid Jews in the attic during the murders in 1942. Ellie Potash, Basia-Ruchel's father, is standing on the steps of a house he owns next door that serves as his leather workshop. *Photo provided by Ryszard Lubinski.* BOTTOM: The "Talmud Torah," Jewish day school, in Trochenbrod in 1935. Don't overlook the two girls who must have sneaked inside while the boys and teachers were preparing for the photograph, and peak through the window adding a note of cheerfulness to the otherwise solemn portrait. Many people in both Israel and the United States provided copies of this photograph, and it also appears in *Hailan V'shoreshav (The Tree and Its Roots: The History of T.L., Sofiyovka-Ignatovka)*, the Trochenbrod-Lozisht memorial book published by the Israeli Bet-Tal organization in 1988.

TOP: A built-in cooking and heating system of the type Trochenbrod craftsmen built for villagers in the region. Heat passed through clay ducts to other rooms of the house. *Photo by the author.* BOTTOM: A procession of Polish Catholics passing through Trochenbrod on their way to the church built for them by Prince Janush Radziwill. Notice the poles set up for telegraph and telephone service. *Photo by Janina Lubinki; provided by Ryszard Lubinski.*

TOP LEFT: YomTov (Yonteleh) Beider at work as a Jewish pioneer in Palestine, 1933. He had arrived from Trochenbrod the year before, and was one of many Trochenbrod pioneers in Palestine in the 1930s. Like many of his friends he discarded his "diaspora name" and adopted a Hebrew name, Chagai Bendavid. TOP RIGHT: The new automobile of the Silno District Administration, late 1930s. This auto would visit Trochenbrod from time to time, and some claim that it was in part to facilitate those visits that the decision was made to pave Trochenbrod's street. *Photo by Janina Lubinki; provided by Ryszard Lubinski.* BOTTOM: A Trochenbrod funeral in the mid 1930s. Rabbi Moshe Hirsch Roitenberg can be seen near the upper left edge of the photo. Photo copied from the book, *Hailan V'shoreshav* (*The Tree and Its Roots: The History of T.L., Sofiyovka-Ignatovka*), the Trochenbrod-Lozisht memorial book, and appears here courtesy of the Israeli Bet-Tal organization.

TOP: Girls performing at a Zionist summer camp in Trochenbrod in 1939. Did any of them survive the slaughter three years later? *Photo by Janina Lubinki; provided by Ryszard Lubinski.* BOTTOM: Ribbon-cutting ceremony in 1939 for the first small section of Trochenbrod's street that was paved. Notice the wooden structures protecting newly planted saplings on the right and left sides. *Photo by Janina Lubinki; provided by Ryszard Lubinski.*

ABOVE: 1939. Young Jewish men and women from Zionist organizations all over East Europe made their way to this shelter, the "Internat," in Vilna (Vilnius) on their way to settle in Palestine. About 200,000 refugees are said to have passed through here. *Photo provided by Hana Tziporen.* OPPOSITE: Trochenbrod's street, 1939. Notice the man standing in the drainage ditch near the upper right edge of the photo. Notice also the bollards on the sides of the street to keep passing wagons away from the ditches, and horse-drawn wagon traffic in the distance in line with the wagon tracks in the upper left. The girl in the foreground is Basia-Ruchel Potash. Less than three years after this photo was taken she hid with her family in the forest during the Nazi slaughters, and was one the few Trochenbrod survivors. But here Basia-Ruchel stands shyly next to her playmate, Ryszard Lubinski, son of the Polish postmistress. *Photo by Janina Lubinski, the postmistress; provided by Ryszard Lubinski.*

ABOVE: A bunker in the forest camp of Medvedev's partisan detachment. The camp was located in Lopaten, about 4.5 miles from Trochenbrod. Nahum Kohn joined this Soviet partisan unit after his own small unit was decimated. The camp has been developed into a museum of partisan activity in the area. *Photo by the author.* OPPOSITE TOP: A scene in Yaromel, 2006. The forest area in the background is where the mass graves of Trochenbrod people are located. OPPOSITE BOTTOM: One of two monuments at the sites of the mass graves of the people of Trochenbrod. *Photos by the author.*

One of two monuments at the site of Trochenbrod. This one was erected in 1992 by several Israelis and an American who were born in Trochenbrod. It's located at what was the north end of town where the synagogue once stood that was burned after the last Trochenbroders were killed. *Photo by the author.*

Photo of a Polish family provided by Betty Gold (Basia-Ruchel Potash). About this photo Betty says, "The man in the center of his family, Yuzef Berdnarski, and his son Yanek, the groom standing in back of him, were the ones who helped us survive. They were angels. We kept in touch with them until they died. My parents sent them packages, medicine, and some money."

בגישה לזכר הקדושים מטרכנוב ולוזישט שנפלו בשנת 26/7-1942.—
2.X.1947 פרנקלד

TOP: Label Safran from Trochenbrod-Lozisht, upper left, and the Ukrainian family that hid him while the Nazis were rounding up Jews for slaughter: the father Davyd Zhuvniruck, and his wife Yaryna and daughter Kateryn. *Photo provided by Esther Foer.* BOTTOM: At the Foehrenwald D.P. camp near Munich, 1947. Survivors from Trochenbrod and Lozisht at a gathering in memory of those who perished. Label Safran is in the middle of the second row. *Photo provided by Esther Foer.*

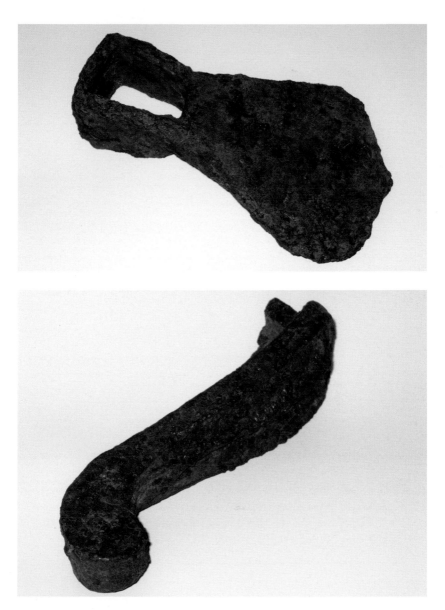

TOP: Head of a short-handled hoe found in the fields of Trochenbrod in August 2009 by cameraman Andriy Dmytruk, and presented as a gift to the author. BOTTOM: A door latch handle found in August 2009 in the area where Trochenbrod's houses once stood. Found by cameraman Andriy Dmytruk and researcher Sergiy Omelchuk, and presented as a gift to the author. A decorative stem with branches and leaves can be discerned running lengthwise down the center. *Photos by the author.*

To this day Trochenbrod's street is echoed in the landscape. The Radziwill forest east of Trochenbrod is in the background. Trees and bushes descended from those that stood in front of Trochenbrod houses remain tenaciously in place in the flat land of the Trochim Ford clearing. *Photo by the author.*

Soviets. Milk, grain, flour, potatoes, and fat were smuggled into Trochenbrod in exchange for clothing, valuables, or money. The trade was carried on at night; being caught meant immediate death. Blacksmiths, shoemakers, and some others were still able to make a living, but many Trochenbroders began starving, trying to stay alive on rotten food and scavenged scraps.

Within four months of the start of German control the recently proud and thriving town of Trochenbrod was reduced to abject poverty, hunger, terror, slavery, extortion, beatings, humiliation, and misery of every other kind— and over this wretchedness hovered the prospect of death consuming anyone anywhere at any time for any reason or no reason. This was the life of the Jews of Trochenbrod, the people of Trochenbrod, until the end of their days.

Trochenbroders who survived the war, or their children, tell of a somewhat mysterious "Dr. Klinger." Late in 1941, not long before the attack on Pearl Harbor and America's entry into the war in early December, this Dr. Klinger, a German Jew living in Lutsk, passed himself off as Gentile. No one seems to know for certain what Dr. Klinger was a doctor of, or for that matter if he was really a doctor at all. He made contact with the Nazi leadership and arranged to employ the Jewish leather workers of Trochenbrod to produce leather goods, especially boots, for the German army. The production was done in Trochenbrod, so the people he could keep engaged as leather workers—as many as possible—were saved from being sent on forced labor crews.

A number of Schutsmen had suspicions about Dr. Klinger, since no one had ever seen him or heard of him before, and some of them had noticed friendly behavior between the German Dr. Klinger and his Jewish laborers. One night in mid-1942, drunken laughter and then shouting was heard from a drinking party Schutsmen were having, and then a single gunshot was heard. In the morning Dr. Klinger's body was found in the street with a bullet through his head. The townspeople buried him as a Jew in Trochenbrod's cemetery.

As winter turned into spring in 1942, it became increasingly clear to many Trochenbrod townspeople that the Germans intended ultimately to kill them all, by slave labor, by starvation, or by outright murder. Some built false walls in their houses or farm buildings and prepared hiding places behind them; some prepared bunkers in the forest; some found ways to obtain false identity papers and began to slip away; and some young Trochenbrod men fled into the forest, as did Nahum Kohn, and began training themselves to be partisans. Most, however—because they would not believe what could no longer be denied, because they clung to hope that their usefulness to the Germans would protect them, because they were certain that God would intervene and save them, or because they could not imagine what they could do about it—struggled to survive, suffered under a heavier and heavier burden of despair, and awaited their fate.

One of the things that is striking in the stories of what took place in and around Trochenbrod as its sun was setting is the degree of barbarism displayed toward the townspeople by Ukrainians, and to a lesser extent Poles, from neighboring villages—and with that, the extraordinary degree of kindness and readiness to put themselves at risk to help their Jewish neighbors shown by quite a few Ukrainian and Polish families. A Ukrainian in the nearby village of Yaromel, for example, told me of his father hiding "a very good person named Itzik" from Trochenbrod in their house for a few days. Then the Germans began searching all the houses very carefully looking for Jews, and it became a matter of mortal risk, so they had no choice but "to say good-bye" to Itzik.

One Trochenbrod survivor told me of a Polish family that hid her family, and later brought food to them where they hid in the forest; and also of Ukrainians who during the winter let Jews hiding in the forest warm themselves in their houses, fed them, and offered food from their gardens. A Ukrainian from the Polish village of Przebradze described a family friend, a red-haired Trochenbroder, who had obtained a false passport that identified him as non-Jewish. He stopped at their house to say good-bye, hid with them for a day, and then continued on to Lutsk to lose himself among the crowds. When the family of Basia-Ruchel Potash hid in the forest, a Polish man who had been her father's customer sometimes brought food to them, and alerted them to dangers. People in the nearby Ukrainian village of Klubochin helped Trochenbrod families survive in the forest and gave support to their young men who formed partisan units.

In preparing for its grisly work, the Nazi murder machine

was very organized and methodical. The plan called for a schedule of exterminations that would leave Ukraine essentially "Judenrein," free of Jews, by October 10, 1942. Accordingly, most of the Jewish people of Kolki were slaughtered on August 9, most of the Jews of Olyka on August 10, and the bulk of Trochenbrod's Jews were scheduled for slaughter on August 11. The Nazis began the process of organizing the mass murder for Trochenbrod with a number of advance actions meant to ensure that everything proceeded efficiently. They and their Schutsmen killed a large number of people in their homes and in Trochenbrod's street, and undertook other forms of terror to reinforce a sense of helplessness, hoping in that way to ensure submission and minimize attempts to escape. They conducted a program of psychological trickery to encourage denial on the part of their victims, not a few of whom to nearly the end believed they were being corralled for labor details.

Chapter Four

DARKNESS

In the early morning hours of Sunday, August 9, 1942, twenty men of *Einsatzgruppe* C, one of the German extermination units, rode into Trochenbrod on motorcycles. In their wake were eleven German army trucks carrying about one hundred Schutsmen. The Schutsmen spread out and ordered everyone to go immediately to the center of town for a meeting where they would be issued labor cards. While pushing everyone, the Schutsmen freely shot people, tens of them, as they moved bewildered to the designated location.

After a long and frightening wait, the German commander

arrived and informed the townspeople that henceforth they would have to live in a ghetto in the area where they were standing, in the middle of Trochenbrod. He told about fifty leather workers and some professionals, ones the Germans wanted to continue working for them, that they must move with their families into a cluster of houses just beyond the north end of town, in the vicinity of the flour mill. Then Einsatzgruppe troops lined everyone up in ranks to count them and determine, according to a formula they used, the depth of pit they would need at a given width and length. People were allowed to return to their homes to gather clothing and other small things for the ghetto, whatever they could carry, but had to be back in the ghetto within two hours.

The Schutsmen lined up along the sides of the street. As long lines of men, women, and children trudged down the street carrying sacks of belongings on their backs, the Schutsmen opened fire from time to time, murdering randomly. They also looked in the houses and dragged anyone they found outside and shot them. Trochenbrod's street echoed with gunshots and the cries of dying people. The goal was now to escape the bullets and get to the ghetto as fast as possible. The ghetto became a longed-for objective. A large number of people dropped their sacks and raced to the forest, using drainage canals for cover whenever they could. Many escaped this way, but many were shot as they tried. For the rest of the day and that night gunfire and cries were heard as the Schutsmen went from house to house hunting Jews and killing them when they found one, and incidentally pillaging. The next morning, Trochenbrod's street was littered with bodies.

That day, August 10, was quiet. There was no life in Trochenbrod except in the ghetto in the center of town and in the barracks of Germans and Schutsmen. People hiding in the forest saw that the Germans and their helpers were searching for them and killing anyone they found. Many calculated that their situation in the forest was hopeless and decided to sneak back into the ghetto at night and take their chances with their fellow Trochenbroders. Many still believed, or convinced themselves, that it was possible that they would be assigned to forced labor crews, and nothing more.

The following day Trochenbrod's Jews were called out of the ghetto houses and were told to prepare for transport: they should bring food for three days with them. They were piled into trucks and taken, group after group, two hundred at a time, to the killing pit in the Yaromel forest about two miles away that Schutsmen had prepared several days earlier—actually several pits, each meant to accommodate single rows of victims one on top of the other. The Trochenbrod Jews were ordered down from the trucks a short distance from the pits, and they approached their destinies on foot in loose ranks. The Germans demanded that everyone undress. One of Trochenbrod's prominent rabbis was in the first row of people that would be shot. He assured the hopeless Trochenbroders that it was acceptable for them to obey the German masters, and he undressed: the Germans immediately shot him, and his naked body collapsed into the pit.

Each few rows of people saw clearly what happened to the rows before, and many became hysterical with terror and despair. Sometimes, as a row of Trochenbrod Jews was pushed toward the edge of the pit, one of them would jump a guard and scream for everyone to run, and others in the row would bolt. Most who bolted were shot, but often a few evaded the bullets and escaped into the forest. Their deaths were only delayed. They were hunted by everyone— Germans, Schutsmen, Banderovtsi, and local villagers. Most were soon found and cut down.

As each row of people approached the pit they had to deposit their rings and money in buckets and place their clothes on steadily growing piles. They were ordered to lie down in the pit, on top of the bodies of those who went before them. Then Schutsmen and Einzatsgruppe soldiers walked up and down the edge of the pit shooting bullets into the backs of the heads of their Trochenbrod victims, just as they had moments before into the heads of the pre-ceding row of the brothers and sisters of those victims. The murderers stepped on the squirming bodies of little children and shot them in the head as well. Late in the afternoon, the first *Aktion* (literally, military operation, but in this case mass murder) was completed. The trucks made a final trip back to Trochenbrod carrying the clothing and other things taken from those who were slaughtered, for temporary storage in the empty Trochenbrod houses.

On that day, August 11, 1942, over forty-five hundred people from Trochenbrod and Lozisht were murdered at the Yaromel mass grave pits. Over three thousand more Jewish people, some from Trochenbrod-Lozisht and many from other settlements in the region, were slaughtered in the forest near Yaromel over the next few weeks.

Tuvia Drori had made his way to Palestine by the time the Nazis murdered his family at the Yaromel pits. In discussing what he heard had happened, Tuvia wondered:

> My mother was a smart woman, hardworking, never complaining, and I don't recall her ever crying or screaming. Did she cry to heaven then?
>
> We heard from a survivor that as the town's head rabbi was led, wearing his prayer shawl, accompanied by his family to the pits, he raised his hands to the sky and cried, "Where is the God who is all-merciful, the supreme justice, the father of widows and orphans? Could it be that the heavens are really empty?"
>
> When I first heard what happened, I also wondered if maybe, after all, the heavens are empty.

Somehow between five hundred and a thousand people remained alive in Trochenbrod's ghetto, and the slave laborers, primarily leather workers, also remained in their small ghetto. At least for the moment the killing stopped. Over the next few weeks the Trochenbrod remnants in the ghetto in the center of town were joined by a steady flow of others who had escaped into the forest, were hungry and exhausted, were being hunted and saw no hope for themselves in the wild, and so returned to the ghetto to share the fate of the friends and relatives they grew up with. In time, the population of the Trochenbrod ghetto after the first *Aktion* grew to about fifteen hundred people. Fifty or more people would sleep in one house. They could not go out. They had no idea what the future held, but they knew well that each day could be their last. They ate the vegetables that still grew in the gardens of ghetto houses and other scraps they somehow gathered. Most were preoccupied grieving for wives and children, sisters and brothers, mothers and fathers, and all the other family members who had been murdered.

Yom Kippur, the Day of Atonement, the most important day on the Jewish calendar, fell on September 21 that year. As the date grew closer, more and more people came in from the forest to spend what they knew was likely to be their last *Yom Kippur* praying with their Trochenbrod friends and relatives. About two weeks earlier, thirty of the leather workers were marched to the Yaromel forest to dig a second set of mass grave pits near the first. While digging the pits, one of them, reportedly the tanner Moshe Shwartz, suddenly rose up and attacked three of the guards with his shovel while screaming to the others to save themselves. Many began to flee into the forest, but most them, like Moshe Shwartz, were killed by German and Schutsmen gunfire.

On *Yom Kippur* the second *Aktion* was completed: almost

everyone in the Trochenbrod ghetto was taken to the second mass grave pit and slaughtered the same way the first group had been slaughtered nearly six weeks earlier. Again, a few remained alive in the ghetto somehow. The remaining leather workers were moved into the largest synagogue, at the north end of Trochenbrod, and continued to work as slave laborers. In December all remaining Jews were taken to the pits and shot. To mark completion of Trochenbrod's eradication in Jewish measure, in human measure, the Nazis set fire to the synagogue where the leather workers had been held—the spot now marked by a modest black marble monument.

Many of Trochenbrod's houses disappeared soon after the families who had lived in them were murdered. The Germans demanded at least one laborer for five days from every household in the surrounding villages to work on dismantling many of Trochenbrod's houses and other buildings. All remaining furniture was removed from the houses and then the buildings were dismantled into building materials. Clothes and furniture were sold to local villagers. Some of the building material was used for local military construction, and the rest was loaded onto trucks and taken to Kivertzy for shipment to Germany to offset shortages there. Later, partisans set fire to some buildings and houses that were left, in order to deny their use to Germans, Schutsmen, or Banderovtsi. After the Germans were driven out by the Red Army in 1944, Ukrainians from the surrounding villages took anything remaining that could be moved, including the paving stones from Trochenbrod's street.

Trochenbrod had vanished.

— —

Of the more than six thousand people in Trochenbrod and Lozisht when the Nazis invaded, possibly as many as sixty survived. These were people who retreated with the Soviets or escaped later across the Soviet border; or people who got hold of false documents and disappeared from Trochenbrod, like the red-haired friend of the woman from Przebradze; or people like Label Safran who were hidden by Polish or Ukrainian families or in some cases protected by an entire village; or people like Basia-Ruchel Potash and her family who fled into the forest and somehow survived there; or people like Chaim Votchin who became partisans before the Nazis could trap them, and did not die as partisans. Many more Trochenbroders initially escaped the mass slaughters, perhaps several hundred, but most of them did not survive the war.

This story of Trochenbrod will end with the voices of three who did survive those last awful days: Basia-Ruchel Potash, Chaim Votchin, and Ryszard Lubinski. They are among the few from Trochenbrod who have stories to tell about that period. Others who witnessed those days were silenced in their witnessing.

The Nazis skillfully took advantage of Ukrainian nationalist sentiments to first turn Ukrainians against Jews and other Ukrainians, and then set Ukrainians and Poles against each other. They stirred up a cauldron of Ukrainian Banderovtsi, Schutsmen, and Communists; Polish self-defense groups and partisans; German army officers of many ranks and units and ordinary German soldiers; and stoked the flames so that innocent Poles, Ukrainians, and Jews—Jews above all—would be consumed in its boiling waters. It is against this background that you should read the following accounts. Every act of defiance or revenge against the murderers and their partners, every help to those defying or taking revenge, every bold move to try to survive, every help given so that some might survive, all these were acts of great risk and heroism.

Basia-Ruchel Potash now lives as Betty Gold in Beachwood, a suburb of Cleveland, Ohio. She was born in Trochenbrod in 1930 and speaks of a delightful childhood there surrounded by a warm extended family, lots of friends, wonderful experiences, rural freedom, and a rich community life. Her childhood suddenly took a downward turn at the age of nine, when the Soviets arrived in Trochenbrod. It turned far more severely and threateningly downward when the Germans took over. But nothing came close to what she and her family endured hiding in the Radziwill forest from the murder and madness the Nazis brought to Trochenbrod. Her story of triumph begins at age twelve:

> My father and his cousin had a big wooden shed in back,
> it was long and narrow; they would store wood and tools

and other things in there. Because of what they heard from refugees from western Poland, they decided—just in case—to build a false wall in the shed, so that if the Nazis come to get us we could go behind the wall and hide. They built it secretly at night.

Later—I remember it was a hot summer day—the Germans and Ukrainians surrounded the *shtetl*, and they took everybody out of their homes. We all had to shlep whatever we could carry, and we had to go to certain houses in the middle of town. This was the Trochenbrod ghetto. I was with my immediate family—my father, my mother, my two brothers, and my father's mother, who lived with us at that time. My other grandmother, she lived across the street, didn't want to go to the ghetto, so she hid; we saw before we left, that they found her and took her out and shot her. They led us to the ghetto, everyone in Trochenbrod I think.

Once we got to the ghetto my family and my father's cousin's family went back to the house, because you were allowed to go back to get some things if you came right back to the ghetto. They left me with my grandmother in the ghetto to watch our belongings. And I sat there with her, and I saw that nobody came back from my family. Right away I thought they must be hiding behind the false wall. And I got scared, and I got angry why they left me. And I was so torn. My grandmother's sitting there with her belongings, and I'm sitting next to her, and all the other Jews were there. I didn't know what to do. I wanted to live, I wanted to go back; she couldn't go back, so I left her. That was a very tough day in my life.

I started running back to our house at the south end of town. As I ran down the street, all the people were walking toward the ghetto, and I was running the other way, and there were the Nazis and Ukrainians with their guns. One of the Germans was busy looking up at something, so I crawled right between his legs, he happened to be standing that way. As I got close to my house I saw there were soldiers in the distance, so I crawled on the ground between the twigs and the bushes along the side of my house.

I got to the false wall, and they wouldn't let me in! They were afraid that the Nazis were using me to find them, so they wouldn't answer when I called to them. I finally started crying, and I said, "There's nobody with me, I'm just alone, there's nobody with me, I'm just alone." I convinced them to open the secret door, and they let me in.

There were seventeen people in that hiding space behind the false wall. Three small children. My cousin's youngest baby was crying. The mother choked her to death; she wanted to save her two boys and the rest of us. We weren't allowed to cough, or even breathe loudly, because Nazis were all over the place. We were holding our mouths; the grownups were stuffing rags and things in our mouths, not to sneeze, not to cough, not to talk.

The false wall was vertical boards. I looked through

a crack between the boards at one point, and I saw they had a truck full of babies. An open truck. Two soldiers that I saw through the crack, they were still leading people to the ghetto, but they were grabbing babies and throwing them by the arm, by the leg, into the truck. And the mothers were reaching for their babies, and screaming. I saw that, and I couldn't understand it, I couldn't understand what it was all about, I couldn't believe it. I saw my little cousin thrown on the truck like a sack of meat . . . how does a child control herself, and not scream and cry when she sees a thing like that? I knew those faces, I knew those babies, I saw them every day of my life. When you're told to be quiet and keep your mouth shut, and you watch that . . . there's nothing we could have done; if I had gone out they would have thrown me in the truck too. I thought, "Maybe they'll just take them to the ghetto, they don't want them to walk, they don't have the patience to wait until babies and toddlers and little kids will get there, so they took them in the truck, and that's how they're transporting them just to the ghetto, and then they'll give them to the parents." No, nothing like that.

A day passed. The next day we heard a lot of shooting. We were still hiding behind the false wall. I did not see what happened, but we heard the shooting clearly, maybe a mile or two away, so we heard it real loud. We found out from a survivor afterward, someone who ran away from the shooting, that they took the rabbi, the parents, the children to a big pit to shoot them. Some ran away, some were shot trying to run away. Some made it to the forest, and when we met them in the forest, sometimes months later, they told us about it.

We couldn't get out from our hiding place the next day because they picked our house to store valuables and clothes they took from the houses and from people they killed. There were so many soldiers there, unloading and packing and moving things, that we couldn't escape. We had to wait through another night and day. The next night, in the middle of the night, we crawled out into a garden that was next to that building. It was raining, we were so grateful it was raining, we hoped nobody would hear us. We crawled to the canals that drained the water: they were long, maybe half a mile. In the canals we crawled to the Radziwill forest, and that's where we ended up.

After a short while things seemed to calm down, and we went back to the ghetto. Almost everybody had come back for *Yom Kippur*. The Germans and Ukrainians surrounded the ghetto, took everyone from their houses and killed them all. How did we get out of it? My father threw us out the window, and yelled, "Run, and we'll meet there and there in the forest." They were the last to get out of the window, after the children were thrown out. My cousin and her husband had two children there—she had choked her third back in the wall; my parents had three children. Her two boys were gunned down: we survived. She was left with none. My parents survived with all three.

Running to the woods through the drainage canal I stepped over my uncle's body, bleeding to death, I stepped over my cousin's bodies, I stepped over my girlfriend's body, I stepped over a rabbi's body. Not just me, but everyone running was jumping over these dead and bleeding bodies of their friends and relatives, some of them screaming for help. My father was yelling, "Run, run, run, don't stop," and we were jumping over dead, half-dead, wounded people we knew, our own flesh and blood, while we were running to save our lives. Can you imagine how we felt, how your heart aches with guilt and pain?

We could still stay in the forest because there were still trees with plenty of leaves. While we stayed there my father and his cousin and a couple of other men who were with us decided they would build bunkers in different spots in the forest to prepare for the winter . . . so if they find us in one spot we'll have someplace else to run to. They dug nine bunkers over a few months. They covered them up with twigs and tree limbs; they would leave a very small entrance where you could just crawl in. So the roofs of the bunkers would look like the forest floor.

While it was warm we stayed outside. At one point my father and the other men decided we should stay in a nearby marshy area where the trees were thick; that would be the safest place. They built a platform from tree limbs over the water, and we lived there day and night. To survive we would go out at night—mostly I would go out, because my brother was circumcised, and if he was caught they could pull down his pants and see he was Jewish. I had a little babushka, and I would go out and find as much food as I could in the yards and orchards of villagers.

In order for me to get back to the family, to find my way back, I'd clap my hands—it could have been some forest animal noise. When I clapped, they'd clap back to me, and that's how they directed me to the platform with the food—apples, or a piece of bread, or whatever I could get. That's how we lived, that's what we ate. For water we used rain water that we caught in a little pot, or sometimes we drank from the swamp even, if it got bad—we could get so thirsty we didn't have a choice. And we just sat there with nothing to do.

At that time there was a Gentile family that my father told about our hiding. We were so hungry, we didn't have what to wear, what to eat anymore, that he figured what have we got to lose, we've got to tell this Gentile family— customers they were, actually—where we were, maybe they'll help us. And they did. When my mother ran away she took with her a few Russian gold coins—she stuffed them in her bosom. In fact, when she fled from the house she had to bribe a Nazi soldier with a gold coin: he took it and let her run, and then he shot at her as she ran. Maybe he missed on purpose, who knows.

So we gave them all the gold we had left—there wasn't much—and they did help us out with a little bread, they would drop off a few packages here and there. We were extremely grateful. It was a life saver for us. And they did not report us, they were loyal and righteous people.

After that, winter set in, and we started to hide in the bunkers. It got to be really very cold. We had with us a coat lined with fur. Don't ask me how or why, but my parents, when they ran from the house in the ghetto, they took with them the gold coins and the fur-lined coat. A man's coat, my father's coat. That was our only protection from the cold, in addition to any clothing we had that hadn't fallen apart yet, and we treasured it. When winter set in it really became disastrous because you couldn't go out for food—your footprints in the snow would lead the villagers to us. If you didn't eat for three days you just didn't eat for three days. You had to wait to walk in a snowstorm or until the snow melted.

One time a really wonderful thing happened: my oldest brother got hold of seven loaves of bread. He stole them from a Polish home. They were baking bread, and he stole them. When he came we almost attacked him, everybody wanted the bread. My dad dug a little shelf inside the bunker, and he stored the breads there. He gave us a speech that it's winter, we can't go out for food now, so this bread's going to have to last as long as possible. Nobody gets more than one piece a day. He showed us the size of the piece for each day with his fingers. In the bunker I was the one lying next to the shelf. I couldn't help myself; I'd pick little pieces of the bread and suck it like a lollypop. I picked and I picked and I picked. The next day they discovered the picking and decided there must be a mouse in the bunker. But then they got me to admit that I was the mouse. So the next day they had me sleep on the other side of the bunker. That bread lasted about a month.

There were nine people in the bunker. We would lie side by side, and if one person turned around everybody had to turn, we were packed that close. It was a shallow dugout: we could sit up, but we couldn't stand up. We were just lying there day and night, looking at each other, hardly talking. And eventually the coat with fur lining got full of lice, so we had to get rid of it. The lice got into our hair—I had very long hair, long pigtails, and my father and cousin both had knives, and they sat down, and they cut my hair off. One strand at a time, they would hold it out and cut it off.

We were cold and we were hungry and we were desperate. We had a little tiny stove of some sort; I don't know where it came from. You could make a little fire. If my brother found potato peelings, you could lick it and stick it to the outside of the little stove, and you could cook the potato peelings that way and eat them.

Of course we got so sick afterwards because they were garbage, we got them out of the garbage or a pig sty and they were smelly, and they were rotten, and then we would throw it all up anyway. But it filled us up momentarily, so we did it anyway.

At one point one of the Gentile people came and we thought it was the Germans or the Ukrainians that had found us, and nobody wanted to go to see who it is. We heard the footsteps right outside the opening. If they'd take one more step they'd fall in on top of us. My younger brother was asleep, and they woke him up and said, "Go see who's there." He didn't know what was going on, so he went to see. He called back, "Oh it's Yuzef." That was our Polish friend. Yuzef came to tell us that he heard in his village that there's a bunker of Jews hiding in the forest, and the Germans are going to come to get them tonight. He came to warn us that they found out about us.

We knew about another group from Trochenbrod who ran away also and were in a bunker about two miles away. So my father went out to visit that family to beg them to let us in their bunker because we had to leave our bunker because they were coming to kill us, and we'd freeze to death if we were outside a bunker. They said no, we couldn't stay there because there was no room, and there really wasn't any room there. My father came back and told us the news.

He said we can't run, enough is enough, whatever

will happen will happen. He sat us down, and he said, "Look, when they come here to kill us, here's what we're going to do: don't wait; get out and run. You'll get shot, but at least you'll be shot on the run. If they find us alive, they'll cut us to pieces." That's what they used to do, the Ukrainans. They used to find women and men in the woods, they'd cut their breasts off, their tongues out, their legs off, and hang them on the trees.

So we stayed there, and we waited, and we were ready to run when they came to kill us. We lay there, and waited, and nobody's coming! All of a sudden we hear shooting. Grenades, and gunshots, terrible terrible sounds. What happened? It was the other bunker that they discovered, the one that had no room for us, and they killed all those people. If they had they taken us in, if they would have had room for us . . .

That was our luck. Go figure it out. A miracle that we survived. We were ready. We were so ready to die that we had all kissed each other good-bye. A funny thing, when my father kissed my mother good-bye he said in Yiddish, "Stay well." We laughed, we really giggled when he said that. If not for a sense of humor I don't think we would have survived, because that's the only thing that kept us going. We laughed at ourselves and cried at ourselves, because we just ran out of emotions.

After that it was so bad, there was so much snow, we couldn't go out. We stayed there because they didn't find us, but we needed food, we needed food. The Polish people couldn't come either because of the snow. We were so hungry, and so cold, so desperate, we had no clothes, our feet were wrapped in leaves. I still suffer because my toes were frozen. My mother would put my feet between her breasts to try to warm them up. My father would blow through his cupped hands on my hands and my feet to warm them. We thought there was still a ghetto in the *shtetl*, and we decided we were going to go; whatever happens to everybody else will happen to us also. That's enough. We can't handle it anymore. No clothes, no food, nothing.

So we get up and we start to go. All nine of us were born in Trochenbrod and knew our way around blindfolded. We were moving toward the *shtetl* and the ghetto through the night. We walked around all night, for hours and hours and hours. My father couldn't understand why he was getting lost, why he couldn't find his way back to Trochenbrod. It wasn't that far; it was only a few miles. First we walked one way, then another way. "I think it's this way; no, it's that way."

We were so exhausted and confused; we were frail from starving and couldn't walk any more. So we decided we'll just sit down in a trench and rest for a while, and when the sun comes up we'll see where we are. While we were sitting there we heard shooting, a lot of shooting. We didn't know what it was. When daylight came we could see the fields behind Trochenbrod houses. We had been close to Trochenbrod and didn't realize it. The men went to find people. They crawled to a house and climbed in through the window, and there was nobody there. They went to another house, and there was nobody there either. We found out later that all the people in the ghetto had been killed before, and the shots we heard were the killings of last leather workers who had been held in the synagogue. Another miracle. We got lost; if we had found our way we would be killed with the leather workers.

I don't know why we didn't commit suicide. Really, nobody wanted to live anymore. We didn't know what to do. We didn't have any strength anymore. We waited till nighttime, and we turned around and went to another bunker. We went there, and we had absolutely nothing to eat. It was already three days. We were starving, literally starving. Our tongues were hanging out, we were pale, we were . . . it's a miracle we didn't eat each other. We picked any leaves we could find, and we ate them, and we usually threw up. We ate snow.

I was twelve years old. I got my period. I didn't know what it was all about. I was lying next to my dad; we were all lying close to each other in the bunker. I woke up, and I was such a bloody mess from my neck to my knees, and my father was also a bloody mess from his neck to his knees. I didn't know if he was bleeding, I didn't know if I was bleeding. Where did it come from? Did somebody choke him? Did somebody kill him? I got hysterical, I started screaming and crying. My mother took me out with my cousin, a lady cousin. They took me under a tree. There was a puddle of water. They washed me up, and they told me about the birds and the bees. I didn't have any social life out there, but they started to warn me about getting pregnant and so on.

There was another bunker not far from us. There was a father, a child, and a few other people, all from Trochenbrod. The little girl wasn't more than three years old. The little girl got very very sick, and she died. They had to leave their bunker because somebody spotted them. And they spotted us. So we all left our bunkers and we left the little girl under a pile of leaves, and we figured maybe the next night, when it all calms down, we'll go and bury her. When we came back to bury her, she was breathing! Just barely. My mother put her on her bosom, and my father was breathing in her mouth, and her father was . . . I mean, it was a scene like not even the movies, it was like animals in a jungle. All the adults gave her drops of water in her mouth, sometimes even spitting in her mouth, and held her close to their bodies to give her warmth, and found pieces of food for her, and . . . and gave her new life. They all together gave her back her life. She survived the war with her father: two out of seven in her family, and she had a wonderful life after the war.

Warm weather finally came again, and we moved to a different part of the forest, because we were afraid that with spring coming shepherds or other people from the villages would be going into the woods and would spot us. We were hearing too many noises, so we were afraid. We went to a bunker about three or four miles away. When the leaves came out we started living out in the open more, and we built a little fire one time. We had no idea, none at all, what was going on outside, even if the war was over or not.

Once we were near a sort of orchard, and the trees were beginning to produce fruit, just the beginnings of the apples, very far from ripe. My brother went out to get those. We were outside the bunker because as I said, there were leaves on the trees already and they were sheltering us. We were looking and waiting for him to come back, and all of a sudden we see horses. There's a soldier on one horse, and on another someone in civilian clothes but with a rifle, and on a third horse another soldier with a rifle. One of them is holding my brother. They caught him stealing the apples. They told him to lead them to where he came from. He was a little boy, and he led them to our bunker. When we saw the Germans, Ukrainians, whatever they were coming toward us with my brother on one of the horses with the soldier, we knew it was the end. We decided as soon as they come with my brother, we're all going to start running. Again we all said good-bye to each other, kissed each other good-bye. We were glad it was over. We didn't even really care anymore.

But it turned out to be the partisans! Russian partisans! Liberation had come! A third miracle! I have never seen such tears and laughter and screaming, and hysterics.

There was such mixed emotions, happiness that the
worst of our hardships was over, that we had survived,
and deep deep sadness about all those who were lost,
who didn't get this far. I looked up at my father and
asked "How did this happen? How did we survive?"
Even as a child, at that time, I couldn't believe it. It made
no sense. We had been living like animals on the run,
like starving animals on the run. Why were we alive?

Chaim Votchin, who now lives in Haifa, Israel, was born
in a village in the vicinity of Rovno. His father died when
he was very young, and his mother remarried and moved to
Lozisht in 1920, when Chaim was six years old. He was an
athletic and strong-willed youngster, one who tended not to
follow traditional paths. He was also very good with mathematics and languages, and from a relatively young age used
these talents as a professional teacher. He had the right set of
inclinations and abilities to be a partisan leader.

One day in 1942, a German soldier ordered Chaim to catch
one of his chickens for the soldier's dinner, and then ". . . stood
there with his chest pushed out and his thumbs in his belt
exploding in laughter" as Chaim chased after the chicken in
his yard. This humiliation cemented Chaim's determination to
prepare for partisan activity. He knew nothing about fighting or
guns or living in the forest, but he began making plans.

Then others came to me, like Gad Rosenblatt, who was
a *Beitar* commander, and we began to discuss how we

could be partisans, where we could get weapons, how we could live in the forest, how we could learn to be fighters, with what could we carry out our fight, how could we get started without the Germans or Ukrainians finding out, and so on. This was much before August 1942. But we didn't go into the forest yet.

We formed a committee and handed out jobs: acquire weapons; convince Trochenbrod young men to join us; make a plan to move Trochenbrod people to the forest; make contact with Russian soldiers who were separated from their units during the big retreat of the Russian army; figure out the best way to get food in the forest; try to contact the Ukrainian Communists. It's very important to find the Ukrainian Communists because they were probably in contact with the Red Army and maybe they get supplies from them; and also we heard their leader is operating in the Radziwill forest and maybe he could tell us how to get weapons.

The name of the Ukrainian Communist partisan leader was Alexander Felyuk. We knew he was from the village of Klubochin a few kilometers through the forest from Trochenbrod. We talked to his mother there, and then met him in the Radziwill Forest. Radziwill had armed forest rangers to protect his property. So Felyuk said, "If you're brave, let's go take the guns from those forest rangers." Alexander Felyuk worked with us for several months and made us into partisans. He was a wonderful man. He died recently, but we stayed in touch with him all these years; we sent him money and packages.

One day one of our boys found a pistol in the Ignatovka cemetery. It was a new pistol, with bullets—it had been left behind when the Soviet soldiers ran away. With this pistol we began to learn how to use guns, and with this pistol we went to a forest ranger, waited until he had to come down from his tower, and then took his rifle.

With one rifle we went into the forest and began to arm ourselves; we got another one and then another one and then another one. We got more rifles and ammunition and even grenades. We became a big enough group of armed partisans. I was the commander and Gad Rosenblatt was my second-in-command. Eventually, including the six Soviet saboteurs we met, we had thirty people.

And so we began to operate. For example, a Jew came to us; he said that a certain Ukrainian found a Jew and turned him over to the Germans. This Ukrainian was called Gapon. Immediately four of us went to Gapon's village and we took him to the forest and shot him.

Another operation: we heard that the Germans arranged to send the animals that were left from Trochenbrod to Germany. We found the herd, ready for transfer to the train station, and we went in and set them free and scattered them all.

Another operation: A very terrible Schutsman who had done horrible things to Jews lived in a small village called Yaromel near Trochenbrod, a Ukrainian village, with mostly straw-covered houses. We pounded on his window: "We are Schutsmen. We have an important message for you. Glory to Ukraine. Open up." The man came and we drank with him. He bragged about all the Jews he killed—this included women and children—and others he gave to the Nazis. Then we showed who we were. His wife screamed and we took him away in a horse wagon that we hired from a Polish man who drove it. We took him to the forest and shot him. The Polish man was happy to be a part of the operation; he was a good man and he had a good time. Revenge felt sweet, revenge for the blood of all the children, women, and men that the Schutsman had murdered.

That's how we started. We didn't know anything about how to fight battles yet, so we started with operations like that.

The Nazis were able to fool so many people. Of course, the nationalist Ukrainians were the biggest fools. They thought they should help the Nazis get rid of the Jewish people and then the Polish people. So they did the work of the Germans with happiness, and when the Soviets drove out the Germans they treated these Ukrainian nationalists as enemies. What is funny, the Nazis saw the Ukrainians as sub-human, good for nothing more than slaves. If the Germans won the war they would take the Ukrainians off the land and shoot them or kill them in slave labor camps.

The Jews also were fooled a lot. Many of them believed the Germans would not kill them even though they saw death in front of them. Once we were planning to attack Trochenbrod and kill the Germans and Schutsmen. We planned to throw grenades into the houses where the Germans and Schutsmen lived, then open fire and kill anybody left. Another group would set fires in different places, burning anything the Germans wanted to have. We sent word to the ghetto to all the Jews saying to sneak away to the forest. Soon one of the Jews from the ghetto showed up and said he was sent to beg that we do nothing. The Jews would not leave. They believed the German promises that there would be no more killings, so they did not want to leave Trochenbrod. We begged them, but they would not listen. Those Jews, they saved the lives of the Germans and Schutsmen. Soon they were murdered by them.

Some Trochenbrod Jews escaped to the forest and stayed there. They did their best in that hard situation. But they suffered. They dug their shelters deep into the ground in hidden parts of the forest. They camouflaged their shelters with loose dirt, tree limbs and leaves. Some shelters they actually built right in the swamps. We helped the families as much as we could. After every raid we brought them food, clothing, and boots. Also we often visited and instructed them how to live better in the forest. That's how far we had come in a month or two—now we were teaching other people how to live in the forest!

In October 1942 one of our partisans, Yosef, came back from a forest nearby after he visited Jews hiding there. On the way to our camp he stumbled on a band of Soviet paratroopers that the Red Army parachuted in to blow up Nazi trains. He really stumbled on them. They were hiding in the bushes and he almost tripped on them. Imagine the tension there was until they figured out how much they could talk together. Yosef told them he would bring the leaders of his partisan unit. They were waiting only a kilometer or two away. We went to meet them.

Their two leaders came toward us. One was a short older man, about forty years old. The other one had light hair and was about twenty-five. They had red stars on their hats and brand-new shiny automatic rifles. When just a few steps separated between us we stopped and for a while we just stared at each other, and then we started to talk. They explained that they were Soviet saboteurs sent to blow up German trains. I told them, "We are a small group, but we are well-organized and we'll be honored to help you destroy the fascists the best we can." The older man took out a cigarette pack from his pocket and offered us a smoke. We told them about our activities, about our hopes, about our men. They asked us to help them with their sabotage, and we agreed. They began to teach a few of us how to blow up trains, and then some of us went with them on missions to blow up trains. And they agreed to fight together with us when we attacked Trochenbrod.

Fall had started. The storks had migrated, and lots of other birds were flying above us to their winter places. The paratroopers and our men who went to sabotage the railroad were successful. They derailed trains almost every night. How things changed! Just a short time ago the Germans were like gods, and now every night they were terrified, at least on the trains. Then the Germans made local villagers help guard the tracks. Each guard had a piece of track that he walked up and down, and a whistle to blow in case they saw something suspicious. A German detachment stood in the train station, ready to move if there was an alert. This made our jobs more difficult but not impossible. We crawled toward the rails, waited for the guard to walk in the other direction, then crawled the last one or two hundred meters, put the explosives where they should go, and crawled away. When a train passed over we exploded the charge.

Alex went away two weeks ago to try to make contact with a group of partisans that we heard rumors about in the forests much further north. Before he came back to us he stopped at his village, Klubochin, where his mother and family were. He learned that the Germans entered the village and rounded up a large group of men, women, and children. They took them to a pit in the forest and murdered them all, including Alex's mother, brother, and little daughter. This was Nazi payment for twenty people from Klubochin, including Alex, who were partisans. They were Communists. The other nineteen partisans were in Klubochin when the Germans came, so they were murdered.

In November we had a big battle with German soldiers. We fought them off. That's how far we had come in two or three months—now we were fighting German detachments and winning! The Germans were surprised that there was an organized group with weapons, and we knew they decided they had to wipe us out. They would come again soon, and this time maybe they would bring Ukrainian militia. What could we do? Should we stay and try to outsmart them? It had begun to snow, and that meant when we went from one of our shelters or storage caves to another one we would leave a trail and "ask" for attack. We also had a problem that we didn't have enough ammunition. Rifles we had, but not enough ammunition. We saw that we couldn't keep going like this. So we decided to leave the Trochenbrod area.

Alex said we should go to the Pripyat swamps in the north, in Byelorussia. Because of what he learned on his travels he was sure there we would find large partisan camps which we could join, and they were receiving Soviet support and Soviet weapons. Our Russian paratroopers did not want to go, they wanted to stay and continue their sabotage work. Although it was Alex's idea to go north, he decided to stay in the Klubochin area, so he went with Medvedev's partisan detachment. This Soviet detachment was based at Lopaten, not far from Klubochin and Trochenbrod. Their main activity was to sabotage high-level German officers and operations in Rovno, which the Germans used as their central administration center.

As we moved north we came across another group of Jewish partisans from Kolki who were also looking for a larger Soviet partisan detachment. We continued north together, and found village after village and town after town where the Jews there were murdered and their possessions were stolen or destroyed. Although I taught Jewish studies, in my heart I was not really a very religious man. But when I saw what happened to the people in Trochenbrod and when I saw what happened in all those other villages and towns and when I heard about what happened in the cities I knew that never in my life again could I even think about a God who saw and heard all this but just sat there watching.

In Byelorussia we found scouts from a Soviet partisan group, and they took us to the base camp of Kovpak's partisan detachment. This detachment was commanded by General Mayov Kovpak, a sixty-year-old fighter from World War I where he fought against the Germans and the White Army. We talked with Kovpak and agreed to become part of his group; we would be a unit of Kovpak's Third Battalion. That night in December 1942, our Jewish partisan group, Trochenbrod's partisan unit, was no more.

One day months later there came a decision from the high command that we should move to the Carpathian Mountains to conduct certain operations there. On the way, we passed through the Radziwill forest. The Jews in Trochenbrod and Lozisht had all been murdered by then. We made up a unit of four hundred raiders to hunt down the Schutsmen and Ukrainian Nationalists who helped the Nazis in their work. We killed many of them and burned their houses.

We decided to burn everything we could that was left in Trochenbrod because we didn't want the Nazis or the Ukrainians to use any of the houses, to benefit from any of the buildings. Jews had owned the flour mill. After they killed the Jews, Ukrainians took over the flour mill. We didn't want them to have it, so we burned it. We took some straw and spread it around, and we spilled fuel all around—there had been fuel there to run the machinery. Then we lit the fire and burned down the flour mill. I tell you that it was sad, but the feeling of revenge was very strong, very strong and very satisfying.

Ryszard Lubinski, postmistress Janina Lubinski's son, was not only the sole non-Jew born in Trochenbrod, he went to school there, all his friends were there, and he grew to the age of twelve there; although he's Catholic, Ryszard thinks of Trochenbrod as his hometown. Ryszard and his mother remained in their home, the post office that was closed down by the Soviets, until the winter of 1942. They were the only ones who lived in Trochenbrod before, during, and after the Holocaust there. He remembers Trochenbrod with deep affection, and he remembers the days of Trochenbrod's descending darkness with great clarity.

Because of Jews, we were in Sofiyovka. Jews made Sofiyovka and developed it into a town that needed a post office, instead of letting it remain a little farming village. My mother came from a town with a lot of Jews and was comfortable among them, and that's why she took the job there.

Also probably because of Sofiyovka Jews, we stayed alive, and I am alive today. Why? When the Russians took over in 1939 they wanted to send us to Siberia because they saw my mother as a Polish official. But the Jews of Sofiyovka said no, and they begged the Russians to let us stay. The Russians talked to the people in Sofiyovka, and then told my mother, "Everyone says that you are a good person and can be trusted, so we will not send you to Siberia, you can stay."

And Trochenbrod's Jews were good to her. For example, she couldn't even get water. Every time she would go out to get water—we had to walk a little bit to bring water from a well—some Sofiyovka man would see her and stop her and say, "No, no, I'll bring the water for you," and they would go to the well, and fill up her bucket, and bring it back to our house. So they respected her and wanted to help her.

The children were learning at the *cheder* every day. All my friends were there in the *cheder*. I had no one to play with, so I'd go and listen under the window of the *cheder*, especially in the summer when the windows were open and I could hear what happened inside. They would learn in Hebrew by memorizing. Since I was standing there listening I would learn by memorizing also, even though I couldn't read and didn't know what it meant. I would just repeat the sounds over and over. One time the teacher called on one of the boys to say several lines. He began reciting the lines, and at one point he made a mistake. That made the teacher very angry, and in the usual way at this school the teacher gave him physical punishment and yelled at him, "Why do you say it wrong?" Sometimes the teacher would hit the pupil's hand with a stick, and sometimes he would hold his mouth open and spit into it for saying a wrong answer. So the boy answered, "Ryszard told me."

But it wasn't true. I knew Yiddish as well as all my friends—I can still speak Yiddish today, especially after some vodka—and from listening at the *cheder* window I knew the Hebrew words better than some of my friends. Sometimes as I was walking in the street, people said, "Look, this is the one who helps the Jewish boys in the *cheder*," because I really did whisper the answers sometimes to help my friends—but always the correct answer. I still remember Hebrew words. Listen: *Baruch atoh adoinoi eiloiheinu melech haoilom . . .*[1]

I remember two oil factories in Sofiyovka, oil presses. One was right after Ellie Potash's house, the other was owned by the Szames family. They were face to face on opposite sides of the street. They had very complicated

1. The opening phrase of many Hebrew blessings.

machinery; it would be in a museum today. Ellie Potash had another house, which was his workshop, next to the post office where we lived. The Jewish school, the *cheder*, was across the street from us, and down a little bit. There was a synagogue a few houses further down, with a very strange rabbi—he was very loud; when he prayed you could hear him everywhere in Trochenbrod.

You know Tevye the dairyman, from Sholom Aleichem's stories? In the introduction to one of his books there is some information that Sholom Aleichem was a tutor of Jewish studies for the daughter of a very wealthy Jew from Sofiyovka who had a lot of land. Sholom Aleichem later married this girl, and the property came into his hands. But he divided it into smaller parts, and finally sold off everything. I always wondered if it's the same Sofiyovka.

I think Sholom Aleichem was in Trochenbrod because behind the house that was the post office where I lived, there was a large field that belonged to one family, that later was divided into small sections. One row of sections belonged to Potash people: Potash, Potash, Potash, one after the other. Another row belonged to Szames people, who were related to Potash: Szames, Szames, Szames, one after the other. So maybe that was the big Sholom Aleichem field divided into smaller parts. What do you think? Is it possible? It could be, because Sholom Aleichem's stories describe the way life was exactly in Sofiyovka.

One time, after the Germans arrived, a strange person appeared in Sofiyovka: Dr. Klinger. He was about fifty years old when he came. To me as a child he seemed very old. He had a lot of scars around his face and on his hands, and some of his fingers were missing. He arrived in Sofiyovka as a German. He dressed in a very elegant way. He seemed to be an important person. The Germans showed him very great respect. He seemed to be a high-level German of some sort, so we wondered where he came from, and where he got his scars and lost his fingers. Was he a veteran from World War I?

He was very often a guest in our house. So we became friendly, and he began to trust us as friends, and he told us he is a Jew. He told us how he got the scars on his face and hands: he was studying somewhere in Germany at the time of Kristallnacht, and Germans attacked him with knives. He protected his face with his hands, and as a result he lost some fingers and has scars all over. The scars let him pretend he was a war veteran, and his wounds brought him a lot of honor among the Germans.

Dr. Klinger convinced the Germans that he needed some of the Jews for something, and protected a lot of them for a while that way. But some of the Schutsmen, Ukrainians, were suspicious about him. They insisted he should come with them for a drink at the end the day once. They got him very drunk. When he was so drunk he was helpless they took down his pants and saw he was circumcised. Then they dragged him to the street and shot him. His body stayed there overnight until Jews came and took him away to bury him the next day.

Before the Germans had the first liquidation they did a preparation of the townspeople. A big-shot German came and gave a speech that no one would be hurt if they followed orders and did not behave wrongly. The Germans were in charge of the town for a long time, and there had been murders, yes, but no mass killing. One day the special liquidation unit of German soldiers arrived in Sofiyovka with assistants of Ukrainian Schutsmen who surrounded the town. No one suspected that they would be killed. They thought, "Oh, another one of the German big-shots will give a speech, and that will be that." So there was no big resistance.

During the first *Aktion* my mother hid sixty people in the attic of the post office. One of my mother's friends, a Jewish woman, and her son were hiding in our house. The boy caught tuberculosis. The Schutsmen went from house to house looking for Jews, but by some miracle they didn't come to our house, so this woman and her son escaped the roundup. But the son got worse and worse. Eventually he started coughing very hard, coughing up blood, got very weak and died. His mother became hysterical. She didn't eat or drink, she just cried. My mother tried to get her to go hide in the attic, but she said she didn't want to live. Then she just walked out the door and started walking up the street. Soon we heard the shot that killed her.

When Russians were in control, the *Volksdeutsch* [Germans] were allowed to leave under a clause of the

Molotov-Ribbentrop agreement. So a nearby *Volks-deutsch* village called Yosefin was emptied of *Volksdeutsch*, and Poles and Ukrainians were moved in there. There was a Polish man in Yosefin, a veteran of war under Pilsudski, a man who knew how to use weapons, a very strong man, and a very commanding person. He was working in his fields on the day of the first *Aktion*. He saw and he heard what was happening. Something snapped in his head, and he became a completely different person, walking around in a daze, mumbling words no one could understand. The next day he put on a coat and told people he was going to search for Free Poland. No one ever saw him again.

More people escaped into the forest from the second killing because it was not so well organized as before—for the Germans it looked easier because so many fewer people meant they didn't have to be as careful. But now the Jews knew what was going to happen so they were better prepared, and more escaped. The beans in the fields behind the houses in Trochenbrod were on tall frames. When running from the Germans, people would sometimes run among the beans because that would hide them, and then they would run in the drainage canals. The second time, one of the young people in the ghetto hid behind the door with an ax, and when a Schutsman entered to call the people out, he chopped him in the neck and almost cut his head off. People felt good that someone showed resistance.

I thought about Trochenbrod often all these years. I

still miss it. I remember eating gefilte fish in Trochenbrod. Since then I've tried it sometimes, but nothing came close to the way it tasted in Sofiyovka. Even when my mother made it, after we came here to Radom, it was not as good as it was when the mothers of my friends gave it to me in Sofiyovka, because that was really in the Jewish style. Whenever I walk in the street and smell cooking of a food like there was in Trochenbrod, I think "Oh, that smells like Sofiyovka," and pictures of Sofiyovka come to my mind. I remember *latkes*—ahh, *latkes*—and *chulunt* in the oven for *Shabbos*, I can smell it now, I can almost taste it. When I think of Sofiyovka I don't think of the slaughter; I think of the life. Laughter, wonderful food, games, happiness, friends, weddings, holidays, warm families.

But I can never forget what it felt like as a child when everybody in Sofiyovka was murdered. When I went for water I saw dead bodies everywhere. Looking down the street of Trochenbrod I saw only empty houses where the families of my friends lived. Where my friends lived, now there was only quiet. The doors and windows of the empty houses were swinging this way and that way in the wind, once in a while hitting the sill with a soft bang, and then with hinges squeaking they starting to swing again. Where are my friends? Where are their families? What happened to my Trochenbrod?

Epilogue

THE STORY CONTINUES

LIGHT[1]

by Yisrael Beider

Don't despair my brother dear,
If in the west day's end seems near.
I beg hold fast these words of mine,
After this darkness a light will shine.

1. This poem, originally in Hebrew, was found among newspaper clippings that Yonteleh Beider had saved. It was written by his brother and probably published around 1939 in *HaKochav* (The Star), a Hebrew-language monthly published in Poland. *HaKochav* published many Hebrew poems by Yisrael Beider.

Trochenbrod, the town that some thought would be a thriving city today, is gone. In the nearly seven decades since its annihilation, what happened to the physical space that Trochenbrod occupied? What happened to the land that might have borne the roads, houses, parks, and buildings of an urban center named Trochenbrod, or Sofiyovka?

After the people of Trochenbrod were murdered, the German army put the land of Trochenbrod and its satellite villages to use supplying food for its soldiers. A *Sonderführer* (an army specialist with a nonmilitary skill) who knew how to run a large farm was brought in, and he established a forced-labor system for people from the surrounding villages to work on the former land of Trochenbrod, now his farm. He had the villagers build him a house near where the last synagogue had been, at the north end of town where today the black marble monument stands. For the house and for several other new farm buildings he had them use materials from dismantled Trochenbrod houses. The *Sonderführer's* farm had horses, goats, cows, and chickens, and the villagers cultivated potatoes, beans, corn, cabbage, and other local crops for the German army there.

The Germans' Trochenbrod farm did not survive more than one growing season. In the fall of 1943, fighters from Kovpak's partisan detachment surrounded the Trochenbrod area and set fire to as many buildings as they could. The *Sonderführer* is said to have escaped to German units near Rovno (Rivne).

Following the war, no one made use of Trochenbrod's land for about ten years. The reasons it was unused before the first Jews settled there 130 years earlier were the reasons it was unused now: relatively poor-quality soil, a marshy lowland, and considerable distance from transportation routes in the region. In addition to that, local villagers already had garden plots near their homes; markets were disrupted by Communist rule; and people were generally without horses or tractors. In short, local people had no incentive—and really no capability—to cultivate Trochenbrod's land.

In the mid-1950s, the Soviets decided they could not leave uncultivated such a large parcel of what had once been farmland. They made modest improvements to prepare the land for farming, and in 1957 assigned the area that had been Trochenbrod and its satellite villages to a collective farm named Nove Zhyttia, New Life. All villages in western Ukraine had undergone forced collectivization by this time, and Nove Zhyttia was headquartered in Domashiv. As Soviet rule lumbered on, a generation was being born in Domashiv and other villages of the area that did not know any life but Soviet life, and had no idea that a town, a Jewish town, had not long ago pulsed where now were only vast hay fields of the New Life collective farm.

In 1971, the Soviet government decided to make some major improvements so Trochenbrod's land could be farmed more intensively. Thirty years had passed since Trochenbrod's disappearance. By this time, few people—and probably no Soviet authorities of substantial rank—knew that a town once stood on this land. One of the major improvements was to build a regional system of drainage canals that included water conduits along what once had been the street through Trochenbrod. That street had shriveled to a scraggly trail among the fields. Because of the drainage system, Trochenbrod's soil was now firmer and the whole area much less sodden, and the collective farm raised rye, corn, wheat, barley, peas, potatoes, and beets, and also grazed livestock there.

On April 26, 1986, the Chernobyl nuclear power plant suffered its well-documented catastrophe. The Chernobyl plant is about two hundred miles east and a bit to the north of Trochenbrod. All the stories I've been told are variants on the same idea, that the Soviet government was committed to supply electricity to Poland from the Chernobyl nuclear plant; in the aftermath of the Chernobyl disaster the government built high-tension lines that transmitted electricity from a power station about thirty-five miles north of Rivne (Rovno) to the Polish market. These lines cut through the area that had been Trochenbrod, and ran parallel to what had been its only street. This infrastructure can be seen in the first photo of the first page of this book's image insert.

Ukraine became an independent country in 1991, and that put an end to collective farms. Cultivation on Trochenbrod land stopped then because, despite its good drainage, the land still was not particularly fertile—people in the area refer to the soil there as "black sand"—and it still was not in ready reach of transportation routes to markets. When you go there today you may find some local people grazing their horses, and sometimes you'll see one or two fields sown in grass or clover for animals. But Trochenbrod's land today remains essentially unused and in government hands. Neither the local nor national government has plans for it. The Trochenbrod area looks today as it does in recent photographs in this book. Few people in the surrounding villages have any idea what used to be there.

And yet Trochenbrod—Sofiyovka—sometimes has a mysterious fleeting presence for local people, almost like the ghost of an unknown soul that still hovers in the air from time to time. Once I was standing in a Trochenbrod field when my Ukrainian friend from Domashiv asked if I'd like to find a keepsake from the town. He said you could often find things at Leah's house. Leah's house? We drove by tractor to what would have been the southern reaches of Trochenbrod and started rooting in the soil near a big fruit tree. This spot is known as Leah's house; no one today knows exactly why. I once walked by a farmer's yard in the area and noticed, snug against the wall of his house, a pile of paving stones that reminded me of the ones I had seen in the photograph of the ribbon-cutting ceremony that appears on page 15 of the image insert. The farmer was working in his yard, and I asked him where he got the stones. "From Sofiyovka," he answered, jerking his head in the direction of where Trochenbrod used to be, as if, "In the next village, over there." A legend circulates that in the first year of this millennium some strangers appeared and dug up a large quantity of gold from the site of Trochenbrod. Children from the surrounding villages who wander out to Trochenbrod's fields sometimes return with pieces of glass from the pre–World War I glass factory, shards of dinner plates, or tools, utensils, or other household objects that hint of life that once was there. There is an acre of land not far from the black marble monument known to everyone as the Shwartz field. Some village young people have never given a thought to what that name might mean; others vaguely guess someone named Shwartz once lived there; old people sometimes retreat into their memories when you ask about it.

For its children and their descendants, Trochenbrod, though it disappeared physically, has flourished in certain ways—lasting community connections and individual prosperity, for example. One cannot say as much for other small towns in the Volyn region, like Olyka, which did not disappear. Olyka had been a vibrant and important administrative and commercial center, where one of the area's principal markets was held each week. Trochenbrod traders were there in force on Olyka market days. It was the seat of the Radziwill family, which had large holdings in the region; I've heard many times the story of the road into Olyka being strewn with rose petals when the prince's son drove into town with his new bride. When I visited Olyka not long ago it was a forlorn and forgotten place of muddy streets and ancient houses. It lacked any but the occasional small rundown shop left over from the Soviet era. Its once glorious brick church stood crumbled like an ancient ruin, and Prince

Radziwill's palace had been converted to an insane asylum from which inmates occasionally wandered out onto the street to hunt for cigarette butts in the gutters. It was a place without past or present, and since any new houses in the area were being built closer to the Lutsk-Rivne highway a bit to the north, it appeared to have no future either.

Trochenbrod has lived on through the power of collective memory. It remained alive first in the form of active groups of émigrés and survivors who identified strongly with their hometown and celebrated the community that it was. Wherever there were large numbers of people from Trochenbrod, they and their families generally flourished. Most of the original Trochenbroders were gone by the end of the 1970s, but after a lull of two or three decades, remarkably, strong ties with Trochenbrod and with each other began flowering again among the children of Trochenbroders, their grandchildren, and their great-grandchildren.

When the war ended, most Trochenbrod survivors found their ways to Displaced Persons camps like Bindermichl, in Lintz, Austria, or Föhrenwald, near Munich, where the photograph at the bottom of page 22 of the image insert was taken. From there survivors went primarily to the United States, Palestine/Israel, Brazil, or Argentina, where there were already large Trochenbrod communities and often even family relatives. There was no sustained contact among Trochenbroders in different countries, though Israeli Trochenbroders did reach out to overseas Trochenbroders during the decade or so after the war. And in 2009 they reached out again.

In Brazil and Argentina there were many Trochenbrod immigrants—in Brazil, especially in Rio de Janeiro, and in Argentina, especially in Buenos Aires and in the provinces of Buenos Aires and Santa Fe—but no formal Trochenbrod organizations. Still, in both countries there was a strong sense of Trochenbrod community. Many immigrants from Trochenbrod were connected by birth or marriage to a small number of Trochenbrod families; they saw each other and helped each other and kept in close contact, as they do to this day, in the context of family interactions and gatherings, and Trochenbrod is always in the room. In the United States and Israel the story was different.

American Trochenbrod families have given me photos, membership lists, bank records, and firsthand accounts of Trochenbrod émigré organizations that existed in Montreal, Canada, and in Baltimore–Washington, D.C., Boston–Worcester, Chicago, Cleveland, Los Angeles, New York–New Jersey, Philadelphia, and Toledo. As Trochenbroders traveled around the country, they would often stay with other Trochenbrod families and participate in local Trochenbrod organization events. These organizations typically got their start ten to twenty years before World War II. They were social organizations where families could reminisce about Trochenbrod and update each other on the latest news from their hometown, but they all devoted themselves as well to raising money for Trochenbrod institutions and families. Most of these organizations fell inactive during or soon after the war, as the letters stopped arriving; some small groups continued gathering into the 1970s.

The Trochenbrod-Lozisht group in Palestine started as an informal community around 1930, and has operated continuously and fairly robustly since then. The center of gravity of the Israeli Trochenbrod community in the early years was Eliezer Burak, who changed his family name to Barkai in Palestine. Eliezer wrote the 1945 article about Trochenbrod quoted on page 69. All new arrivals from Trochenbrod, including my father, stayed with Eliezer and his family until they found a job and a place to live in Palestine. When survivors arrived after the war, Eliezer quizzed them about what happened to different Trochenbrod families, and then passed information about survivors to Jewish soldiers operating in Europe. In that way, a number of survivors were tracked down, including those in D.P. camps and children whose doomed parents had paid Ukrainian families to protect them, and arrangements were made to bring them to the Trochenbrod community in Palestine. Eliezer also wrote to Trochenbroders in Brazil, Argentina, and the United States for money to help support and integrate survivors who arrived in Palestine. Later he was instrumental in organizing construction of the Trochenbrod and Lozisht synagogue and community center in Israel, known in Hebrew as Bet Tal. Eliezer Barkai served as the contact point for Trochenbroders worldwide, and for years maintained regular contact with many of them.

By 1959 Bet Tal had been built near Tel Aviv, and the

Trochenbrod community established a formal nonprofit organization, the Bet Tal Association. In 1988, one of the Bet Tal leaders, a Trochenbrod native named Tuvia Drori (quoted on pages 81 and 105), finally managed to travel to the site of Trochenbrod, in Soviet territory. He couldn't relate to the terrain of the region and had trouble finding someone who knew the site, but he did eventually find a villager who took him there on his horse-drawn wagon. Tuvia returned to Israel shaken by the experience of seeing nothing but an empty field where his town had been and nothing marking the mass grave. In 1992, the Bet Tal Association installed black marble monuments at the site of Trochenbrod and at the site of the mass grave. Over the next fifteen years they organized three visits to the site of Trochenbrod and worked hard to include as many young descendants as possible. In 2007 they established a Web site (http://Bet-Tal.com); in that same year the Israeli Bet Tal Association decided to work toward becoming an international organization, a focal point for Trochenbrod descendants worldwide. They kicked off this effort with an international gathering of Trochenbrod natives and descendants, at the site of Trochenbrod, in August 2009—over sixty-five years after Trochenbrod and its people perished.

Before telling you about that remarkable event I want to turn the clock back a bit to catch up with Basia-Ruchel Potash, the young Trochenbrod girl who survived by hiding in the forest with her family, and her friend Ryszard Lubinski, son of Trochenbrod's postmistress. They are pictured together in the photograph on page 16 of the image insert. Basia-Ruchel and her family ended up at the Bindermichl D.P. camp, and in 1946 immigrated to the United States, to Cleveland, where they had family. In due course she married, raised a family, and had a successful professional life as Betty Gold. Ryszard and his mother left the ruins of Trochenbrod to work in another town in the region, and then made their way to Radom, Poland. Ryszard eventually became a construction engineer in Communist Poland, and today is retired in Radom, not far from his children. It never crossed the mind of either that the other might still be alive.

In 1996, the Shalom Foundation, in Warsaw, published *And I Still See Their Faces: Images of Polish Jews*. This is a book of beautifully printed photographs of Polish Jews before the Holocaust. The photos were selected from thousands sent in by Poles who in many cases had known the people in the photographs. Often they attached comments about their photograph. The book was not distributed in the United States at that time, but an exhibit of photographs from it was mounted in Detroit two years after the book was published. By chance, the *Cleveland Jewish News* reported on the Detroit exhibit. Betty Gold always read the *Cleveland Jewish News*. Ryszard Lubinski had sent in one of the photos taken by his mother, the one that appears on the top of page 15 of the image insert of this book. Although Ryszard's photo was selected for *And I Still See Their Faces*, it did not appear in the article. Yet, one might think miraculously, the comment that Ryszard sent along with the photo *did* appear in the article. It read:

I was born in 1929 and, for 12 years, was brought up in Zofiówka in Volhynia. The town had a population of about five thousand residents, almost all of them Jewish. Yiddish language and Jewish customs also became part of my everyday life. After the Soviet invasion, when the Jewish language became the language of instruction at the local school, it did not hinder me, a Pole, in my studies. Afterwards, the Germans came. In August of 1942, almost the entire population was murdered in the nearby forest . . . Zofiówka suddenly ceased to exist.

—*Ryszard Lubinski, Radom*

Betty Gold read this on Mother's Day 1998. She read it again, and again, and again. Her eyes blurred over with tears and she felt happiness, intense excitement, and a sense of miracle in one overwhelming emotion; she couldn't contain herself. I know this because she called me to declare that she had just received the most wonderful Mother's Day gift ever. She tracked down Ryszard's phone number and called him. They talked excitedly in Yiddish and Polish, and a few months later they met, in Radom, after more than half a century had passed. They have been in regular contact ever since, and that led me to Radom to ask Ryzsard for his recollections for this book. While interviewing him I asked if he would like to join the group planning to visit Trochenbrod in August 2009. He said no: he has wonderful childhood memories of Trochenbrod, and he would not like to upset those memories by seeing nothing there but the mass grave.

In 2002, Jonathan Safran Foer published his novel *Everything Is Illuminated*. That book and the movie with the same title kept Trochenbrod's name current for several years. Even though the book and movie use the variant "Trachimbrod," people descended from Trochenbrod knew what it was. Many of them had known of Trochenbrod only as family legend, sometimes handed down with diminishing clarity over several generations. They were amazed to learn that other people knew of Trochenbrod, they were excited by its new fame, and they wanted to know more about the town and connect with other Trochenbrod descendants. Their interest in reconnecting stirred for two or three years and then, one might again think miraculously, bumped up against the Israeli Bet Tal Association's wish to reach out to Trochenbroders worldwide.

An effort to put together a contact list of Trochenbrod families in 2008 quickly made clear that thousands of people in the United States felt connected to the town. What began as an idea for an unadorned gathering of a few Trochenbrod families in Washington, D.C., ended up, as a result of clamor across the country, as a national Trochenbrod reunion. One hundred forty people came from all corners of the United States. Trochenbrod gatherings in Los Angeles and Rio de Janeiro took place in the following months. The Bet Tal Association began organizing an international gathering at the site of Trochenbrod.

On August 18, 2009, three Trochenbrod natives—two who survived in the forest and one who slipped away during the Russian occupation—and seventy-five descendants of Trochenbroders, the youngest among them teenagers, gathered in the Ukrainian village of Domashiv. They had come from Brazil, Canada, Israel, Ukraine, and the United States. They made their way in a procession of fifteen horse-drawn wagons through Domashiv farm fields and then through abandoned acreage to the site of Trochenbrod. They deliberately traveled using the same means of transportation that their ancestors had used.

One who survived in the forest was Betty Gold, Basia-Ruchel Potash, who told her story of survival in Chapter 4 of this book. Another was Evgenia Shvardovskaya, whose story is summarized starting on page 182. Evgenia is frail, but her grandson, who heads the small Jewish community in Lutsk, came back to Trochenbrod with her and helped her. The one who slipped away before the Germans came was Shmulik Potash, whose story of escape is told in Chapter 3. With their first-person stories, these people were able to bring Trochenbrod alive for the rapt descendants visiting Trochenbrod. Shmulik strolled the entire length of Trochenbrod's street pointing out the locations of shops, public buildings, and the homes of individual families. People scooped up soil that had been beneath the houses of their forebears, and searched in the ground for signs of their families' lives. They conducted a ceremony at the black marble monument at the north end of Trochenbrod, and then an even more moving one, with songs, stories, and prayers, at the black marble monument at the mass grave. They discovered a visceral connection to this place, a sense of identity with this vast field somewhere in Ukraine that they had never seen before. They discovered within the group relatives from other countries that they had never met, and in some cases had not known existed. They felt a kinship with each other that left them singing and laughing together as family.

The proceedings were in English and Hebrew. The Ukrainian wagon drivers, who brought their horses and wagons from neighboring villages, and some Ukrainian friends and well-wishers from Domashiv and Lutsk, watched respectfully, though they understood nothing. Yet the looks on many of their faces said they understood everything; some had tears in their eyes. Later they told me that the idea that people came from all over the world to meet each other, make family connections, visit the graves of their ancestors, and recapture the history of the place moved them deeply, and was a lesson for them. Now they wanted to know more about the history of the area, not just the history of Ukrainians. It was the first time they fully understood—or remembered—that many different types of people had lived in the area and made up its history. Imagine, there was a Jewish town here! They wanted to know more about those people and how they lived.

WITNESSES REMEMBER

S ome recollections of people in this appendix appeared
earlier. What follows are additional memories that
further enrich one's sense of what Trochenbrod was
and what took place there.

Shoil Burak

One thing many Trochenbrod natives remember clearly
about Trochenbrod is mud. Because Trochenbrod was established in a marshy lowland area, the street through town
became impassible to wagons after a rain. Shoil Burak was
born in Trochenbrod in the late 1870s; he immigrated to the

United States in the early twentieth century. He reminisced to his family a sentiment, as captured by his granddaughter Alyn Levin-Hadar, that other Trochenbrod families reported hearing from their immigrant forebears as well:

> When it rained, I'd be up to my knees in mud. Mud and dirt—these are my most vivid memories of Trochenbrod. We found excuses to take baths because of the mud. You ask would I would want to return to the old country? Not to all that mud and dirt—I'm an American now.

In America, Shoil used to tell his children made-up bedtime stories set in Trochenbrod. Although the stories were made up, they nevertheless somehow always included in them a reference to "blota," Yiddish for mud.

— —

Mikhailo Demchuk

Mikhailo was born in the village of Yaromel, near Trochenbrod, in 1932. He lives there with his family even today. I spoke with him in 1997, and again on several of the later trips I took to the area. Mikhailo had clear memories of Trochenbrod and the war years.

> A lot of people used to go to Sofiyovka because they wanted to buy different things for their houses, and clothes. There were shops selling shoes, clothes, a

bakery—they baked a lot of kinds of bread—leather, mills. The merchants in Sofiyovka really trusted us: they gave us things without money, because they knew we'd give it to them when we had money. If Sofiyovka had survived, it would be a big city by now.

There were good house-builders, good painters, and very good specialists of all kinds, especially related to construction and house repair, that would work in all the villages around here.

There was a Jewish family that that we knew in Sofiyovka, and they had kids, and I was friends with them. We used to play together: a girl, Esther, and two boys, Yoshko and Itzik.

In Sofiyovka there were a lot of geese, and the people had good houses, mostly new ones but some older ones. Wealthy people there had better houses, people with less money had simpler houses. On the whole, it was more or less like our houses—not exactly the same, but similar. There were trees along the street. Also, a lot of the houses had fruit trees on their land: cherries, pears, apples. . . . Everybody had a piece of land there, and they worked on it. It was a nice town.

To make some money young girls and ladies from villages like Yaromel would go to Sofiyovka to help people with the fruit, with their gardens, and around the house. Everyone was happy with that arrangement. It was a good time, but then it changed.

Before the war there were really good relationships

between the Polish people, the Jews, and the Ukrainians. Relations between the Jews and Ukrainians were probably better than the relations between the Poles and the Ukrainians. But everybody was friendly with everybody. For example, there were lots of Polish houses in Yaromel. But after the war started, something happened: Polish and Ukrainian people attacked each other; everybody became enemies.

Of course, I was very young during the war, but I remember seeing trucks filled with people being driven past our house into the woods, hearing shots, and later seeing empty trucks return. Day after day they drove past my house. When things began to heat up for us we prepared to run away. We ran away to the nearby village, Mikove. But my father was killed by Polish people there. They saw we were running away so they attacked us, and only I and my two brothers survived, with nothing. We came back and found Yaromel burned down: only two houses left, and the little lake. So we were really very poor.

Ukrainians and Poles attacked each other and Jews. There were three armies, German, Ukrainian, and Polish, and they were attacking each other. Those Polish people who attacked us came from Przebradze, a Polish village not far from here.

— —

Tuvia Drori

Tuvia Drori was born to Trochenbrod's Antwarg family in 1918 and fled for Palestine in the autumn of 1939. He now lives in Givatayim, just east of Tel Aviv, Israel.

When the Polish came back for good in 1921 and 1922 they took Jews for forced work. They came to take my father on *Shabbat*, and he refused to go. My father work on *Shabbat*? So they beat him, and I remember well as a child the horror of watching my father being beaten— that's stayed with me all my life; I can see the image clearly before my eyes today. My father would never work on *Shabbat*. My father went to America, but found he had to work on *Shabbat*, so he came back, and stayed in Trochenbrod to the end.

In 1988, when I went back to Trochenbrod the first time, I found the two mass graves. I saw a small monument with a fence around it. On the monument was written that here were buried the people murdered by Nazis, from Trochenbrod and Lozisht. It was very emotional for me: I fell to the ground and cried.

When I returned to Israel, no one believed what I had seen; and anyway, they were afraid to go to Russia. A year passed. Then a few of them went, and it opened up, and then people started to go from other towns in the area— Lutsk, Kolki, Olyka—to visit and set up monuments. We arranged for the monuments to be built there in Ukraine, working with the head of the local council. It was a joint undertaking. I was the chairman of Bet TAL at that time. A committee of people organized it here in Israel: Anshel Shpielman, Gad Rosenblatt, others . . . not me alone.

— —

BETTY GOLD

Betty was born Basia-Ruchel Potash in Trochenbrod in 1930, and spent the first twelve years of her life there. She fled into the forest with her family during the mass murders in August and September 1942. Betty now lives in Beachwood, a suburb of Cleveland, Ohio.

Everyone in Trochenbrod was Jewish except the postmistress, the gentleman who sold schnapps, and another gentleman who was busy doing things for the Jewish people they were not allowed to do on *Shabbos*. We were surrounded by Polish and Ukrainian villages. It was a one-street *shtetl*. Everyone knew everyone and everyone was related to everyone, and we all lived very close to our aunts and uncles, just crossing the street or walking next door to them.

I remember my grandparents on my father's side very well. But my mother's mother lived alone across the street—her husband died many years earlier. We used to love to go there, to my grandmother's house, and sleep there and live with her, and so on. I had two brothers, Shimon and Baruch, both older than me.

My mother had a very nice life. They considered her

the society lady in Trochenbrod. She was involved in *Beitar*, she was involved in Jewish organizations, and she would write some plays, and she was always very very well groomed. She was very beautiful, and she always took a great deal of pride in how she presented herself to the people in the *shtetl*. She never worked, because my father really provided well for her, she didn't have to. I don't remember any women working in the *shtetl* when I was a little girl, at all—unless they helped their husbands a little bit in his business.

My father worked in his business. I loved my dad a lot. We used to go together on the way to school, and he'd go to the shop, and I'd continue on to the school— and stop in the bakery on the way and buy a *kichel* [sweet cracker] and put it on my father's bill. We had a pretty decent life until the war started.

The best part of course, was when all the families would be together, and visit, and go to the park on *Shabbos* afternoons, and sing the *Shabbos* songs. The house would light up on Friday night, before *Shabbos*. Everybody would be bathed, and dressed, and candles were shining.

I used to sing at the weddings when I was a little girl. They would be outside, and the whole *shtetl* would come. I don't know why they picked me to sing a song or read a poem for the bride and groom. I really loved the weddings. I also participated with my brother in a lot of children's plays at school as well as in the *Beitar* organization.

We had lots of cousins. A cousin wasn't a cousin,

like here; a cousin was a sister or a brother—there was no difference. We lived together, we slept often together, and played together, and went to school together. We didn't know the difference between sisters or brothers or cousins.

At least twice a month, every other Friday, I would go with a girlfriend of mine, and we'd both carry a basket. We'd go house to house, we'd collect baked goods and pastries and candy or whatever one could give, and we'd take it to the poor people. I started doing that when I was a very little girl; a lot of children did that in our *shtetl*. Of course I'd always steal from the things that we gave from our house, because when we started we had a lot from our house already.

In Trochenbrod there were no cars. There were a lot of merchants who had horses, and they would go to markets—there were a number of markets in different towns in the area—and they would sell cattle or buy cattle, or sell fruit and vegetables or buy fruit and vegetables; they were traders. That was a big big thing, going to market, for quite a few people in our town.

Everyone worked the land. They had big gardens, acres and acres. So besides providing food for their families, they had a lot to sell in the market, and make money this way. And also a lot of people had cows, and the milk would be picked up to make butter and cheese and so forth; so they made some of their living from that. We had a goat, and I had chickens, and I even had a horse at one time that I loved to ride, no saddle of course.

When I was little there was no electricity in our shtetl and there were no paved roads. And then, toward the end of the 1930s, they were paving the road, we had some electricity, and the town was beginning to develop more and more and more. Communication began to happen. Everybody read the *Forward* and talked politics. My father bought a radio. The first radio in Trochenbrod! That was so exciting; everybody came to see how it was being installed. There were big wires strung above and then going into the ground; I remember men working on it. We also had a phonograph, a wind-up phonograph.

I remember hearing Polish music on the radio. And then the President of Poland, Yuzef Pilsudski, was making a speech of some sort. I don't remember what he said, of course, but I remember hearing people saying, "Ooh, Yuzef Pilsudski is going to speak, Yuzef Pilsudski is going to speak," and that's when I learned the name Yuzef Pilsudski.

My eighth birthday party, I think it was my only birthday party. My little friends came. One brought me a bobby pin for a present, and another brought me a ribbon, and another one some pretty colorful rubber bands. Can you imagine that today? Bobby pins and ribbons and rubber bands? But it was so exciting . . . I was more fond of that than if I would get today a thousand-dollar gift.

Once my father brought a rabbi—I don't remember from what city he was—but he was a very famous rabbi, a scribe, and we put him up in our house for a few weeks. My father dedicated a Torah scroll to the *shul* [synagogue], and this scribe was there writing it. People would come and donate what they could and the scribe would write a sentence or a paragraph in their name. It meant a great deal to everyone. My father put me on top of the closet, an armoire they call them now, and I'd watch the people as they came into our house and make their donations. I watched the people coming and going, but I didn't understand what it was all about. Then the rabbi—I can see him with his big round fur hat and long beard—explained it all to me. That was very special.

We knew about Easter and Christmas. You could go into the postmistress's house, and they had a beautiful tree at Christmas time. They would come and buy things for the holidays—my father's shop was right next door to the post office. There was one little play I was in at the Polish school where I played the part of an angel. I don't remember what it was about, but it was Christmastime.

The postmistress's son was a friend of mine. They'd invite me at Christmas to celebrate with them. We were good friends with them. I remember going to his house and seeing the Christmas tree and thinking it was so beautiful, so much fun with all the ornaments and everything, and the house was decorated, and we had cookies. I liked it, but I knew it wasn't our holiday. Maybe I didn't even know it was a holiday; just a celebration of some sort. Anyway, I knew it had nothing to do with us. It was just fun.

—-

Betty Hellman

Betty was born Peshia Gotman in Trochenbrod in 1921. She left when she was nearly eighteen years old, in late 1938, after the paving of Trochenbrod's street was well under way. Betty now lives in Pittsburgh, Pennsylvania.

We would go on the postal wagon to Lutsk. Once there were ten of us. The driver made a few of us get off because the horse couldn't pull so much. So we took turns, and all the way to Lutsk we were jumping off and on the wagon.

The best thing about spring was that the mud dried up, we didn't have to deal with the mud. Many times, walking to school, we fell in the mud, with the books even, and we couldn't get up.

Our biggest entertainment was going into the forest to pick things. We used to go Saturdays, mostly . . . they had there blueberries, and they had cranberries in the woods. But God help you if the guard, Radziwill's forest guard in a uniform, comes. He'd hit you with his big stick; we had a big pot tied on the waist to pick and throw berries in it, and you had to go shhhh, so he wouldn't hear that we're there, and sometimes they chased us out. But, you could get a ticket! You paid, like, five zlotys, and you were allowed to pick berries. But who had five zlotys to give them?

In the fall was like here, it was chilly, and leaves were falling, the wind was blowing, and people were getting ready for the winter.

The winter was miserable. There was a lot of snow in the winter. I remember when I was laying in bed I was able to write on the wall because it was snow, it was frozen on the wall, but you could write with your finger.

How we prepared for the winter, you know what they used to do? They used to dig a hole in the ground sometimes, and put in potatoes, and fill it with straw . . . we had to prepare for our animals; we had a cow, people had horses. You had to have hay, you put it in a little building in back. Our cow stayed in the back part of our house. Because of that, I don't like milk . . . it wasn't very clean. Some people had root cellars. We had that in our house. You'd open up a door in the floor of the house to get to the cellar. We'd have to get the hay in, and put it over the rafters.

I would say it was like, like a whole Jewish town. It was like the forest had wrapped its arms around the town. And I always used to say it had to be a street torn away from some city, and then landed there. Because it was one street, but nothing around it, behind it; just one street all of a sudden, and you call it a town. So I used to say that this street must have been blown away from some city and landed there.

It didn't have just little shops. It had some pretty nice stores. Nice dry goods stores, clothes, material, two shoe stores, butcher shops, grocery stores a few of them, a dairy—we would give them milk from our cow, and they made butter and cheese; they sold butter in Lutsk once a week. There were tanneries that made leather from the raw skins. Avrum Bass opened up a real bakery shop in town. They were pretty well off, they were doing OK.

There were a few people that were rich, and I'll tell you why. There was a family by the name Antwarg, and they lived in a very nice big home, that I never was there, I never saw inside it. It had a big fence around it. They had a very beautiful daughter that was very well known in town, and they had money because . . . some of the families, the husband would go to America, make a little money—some of them never came back to their wives, they found different women in America—and some of them came back with a few dollars. But after a few years, five years, the dollars were gone.

My older sister married a fellow like this. He had no profession, and if he had a profession what would he do with it there in Trochenbrod? She was a poor girl, my mother had six girls, and her husband died when I was eighteen months old. I was born nine years after the last bunch. So he died and left her with lots of kids, but some of them, their husbands came to America, and they made a few dollars, and my sister married one of the sons whose father came back. He was dressed nicely, with a collar and a tie . . .

I went to Lutsk many many times: not so much to buy, no—I couldn't afford something like that, it was out of the question. I went to Lutsk a lot when I was trying to get to America; the administrative offices were there. And I had very good friends there, elderly people, through marriage we were related. So I was in Lutsk a lot; I knew the city very well, and made a lot of friends there.

We had our own theater in Trochenbrod; I was in many plays in Yiddish. We had plays around all the holidays. In the Polish school we also had plays, but they were in Polish. I remember Nachman Rotenberg was the wolf when I was Little Red Riding Hood. Tuvia was also one of my friends.

—–

IDA LISS

Ida's story has an unusual twist. She was born in Chicago in 1912 to parents who had immigrated separately from Trochenbrod, and then met and married in the United States. Her father was from the Gilden family and her mother from the Kerman family. They went back to Trochenbrod in 1912 to visit their families and show off their nearly one-year -old child. They stayed on a bit, then were caught there by World War I, and then stayed longer. Ida eventually returned to the United States. with her mother in 1928, when she was sixteen years old. She is the only person to have grown up in Trochenbrod as a U.S. citizen. Ida now lives in Evanston, Illinois, just north of Chicago. She says that these days she spends more time in Trochenbrod than anywhere else—she sees it in her dreams most nights and remembers it clearly and with affection in her daydreams.

If I was able to go to Trochenbrod now, I'd point out to you where I lived. I can just see my house where I lived. And where my uncles lived: one uncle lived on one side of us and one lived on the other side. One uncle had a granddaughter named Baske. And Baske had a love affair with a Blitzstein; I don't know if they ever got married or not. But every Saturday he used to come there for lunch; and I used to see, she put powder on, and lipstick, and made herself look beautiful. She was a gorgeous girl, but she used to do all that stuff, and I knew he was coming.

The main street was nothing but a long road of dirt. It wasn't bricks, or wood, or anything, nothing but mud. And on each side of the street was like a ditch where the soldiers used to hide in there. And they had a board over that; if you walked you walked on the board, not a sidewalk, there was no sidewalk. And in the middle was enough for a horse and wagon to go through; there was no cars, only horse-and-wagons—in the mud.

We lived there in a white stucco house. That was my grandmother's house. Baba Rivke, it was her house; we lived in her house, a white stucco house. Everybody had a backyard. It was as big as like, maybe 25 by 125. A big-size lot; everybody had a lot that big. And we used to grow potatoes, and vegetables, and everything they could grow in the backyard.

We lived in the middle of Trochenbrod. One side was north Trochenbrod and one side was south Tro-

chenbrod, and we were like in the middle of Trochenbrod. If I was there, I could walk right up to the house
and show you which house I lived in.

When I go to sleep, what do you think I do? I don't
watch television, I can't see it, I don't even turn it on. So
what do you think I do? I dream about things from my
life, like Trochenbrod. I can see, I can see . . . I can see
Trochenbrod right in front of me.

—–

RYSZARD LUBINSKI

Ryszard Lubinski is the son of Trochenbrod's Polish postmistress. This was a government job that Jews were not permitted
to have. Ryszard's mother took the job because she needed
work and because she grew up in a western Polish town with
many Jews, knew their ways, and was comfortable among
them. After arriving in Trochenbrod she fell in love with the
forest ranger of the Lopaten Forest, where during the war
Medvedev's partisan detachment would be based, and married him. The couple separated while Ryszard's mother was
pregnant. His mother was joined by her sister to help run the
post office, and she helped also with Ryszard's birth in 1929.
Ryszard grew to age twelve in Trochenbrod, among its Jewish
families, Jewish children, Jewish food, Jewish customs, and
Jewish languages. Today Ryszard lives in Radom, Poland.

I went to the Polish public school in Trochenbrod

together with my Jewish friends. I was living in Sofiyovka until winter 1942, until the *Shoah*[1] there took
everything. I was twelve years old when we left.

Toward the end of the 1930s, long after my mother
and father were separated, my mother was a young, attrac-
tive, well-educated woman about thirty-five years old. She
was looking for friends of her general age and type, and in
Trochenbrod that meant Jewish girls. Jewish girls from Sofiyovka, or later, from elsewhere. When the Russians reorga-
nized the educational system to ten grades instead of seven
as it was under the Polish government, they needed more
teachers for more classes, so many Jewish teachers arrived
from other places to work in the Sofiyovka school. These
people were a society for my mother because they were a
similar age and education. Many of these teachers lived in
our house because when the Russians came they shut down
the post office and we had extra space in the house.

Once a rich Russian named Lenko discovered mineral
waters at Zuraviche, which was not too far north from Sofiyovka. A small hotel was built there for people who would
come for the waters. I heard that later the Soviets organized
it into a big resort. There were people from Sofiyovka who
worked in that place, at the baths. Because my mother
was the head of the post office, she was often invited to
big events there, together with the police chief, as a Polish
official person. My aunt, my mother's sister, worked there

1. Hebrew for "Holocaust."

after the post office was closed. She would steal food from there, and that's how we ate in those days.

Chaim Veitzblum was one of the teachers that lived in our house, with his wife. He had run away from Olyka. He was a very talented teacher: he could sing, he played an instrument, he painted, and he taught mathematics. My mother and another person created false documents for him, so he became Albin Ostrovsky. A year later, after we left Sofiyovka, he visited us in a village where we stayed for a time. He was driving a farm wagon, and he had a big mustache, and he had changed his character, and he looked and acted just like a rural peasant. The trick saved his life. I wonder if he's still alive somewhere.

In 1943 the Germans found a way to protect their backs by telling Ukrainians to attack and destroy Polish people in the area around Sofiyovka, because the Polish people living there saw themselves as Polish citizens generally against the Nazis. Little Polish villages spread around the area suffered from armed Ukrainian groups, who destroyed those settlements completely— they burned the houses and killed the people. So Polish people decided to build fort areas that they could defend from the Ukrainians. The fort areas were built from Polish villages, and then people from other villages came inside them. The big number of Polish people in these fort areas could defend themselves from the Ukrainians.

There was a Polish village on the way to Lutsk, Prze-bradze, which was made into the first fort area. There were about eight hundred people in that village before, and at the end, after it was a fort area, about twenty-five thousand Polish people were there. After all the killing in Sofiyovka some scouts from Przebradze found several Jewish families hiding in the Radziwill forest. They took them and some others who were hiding in a marshy area of the forest back with them to Przebradze. I know one of them was the tailor from Trochenbrod and his family. All these Jews were protected in Przebradze until the Germans left.

Generally, Jews didn't drink alcohol much. Of course, in all of Sofiyovka and Ignatovka I'm sure there were a few who got drunk from time to time—for example I remember the barber liked to drink a good bit—but generally you didn't see drunk people on the street. Even on Jewish holidays . . . and this was unusual because on Christian holidays, especially Ukrainian holidays, everyone would be drunk—they'd drink a lot of vodka and be drunk in the street. And the Jews, maybe they drank on their holidays, but you never saw them drunk.

There were very few other Polish people in Sofiyovka. Those who were there were good people—not influenced by any ideology or philosophy or anti-Jewish politics. These people, like the constable, had decided to live among Jews, so they lived among Jews. Everyone had good relations with Jews, but I was the only non-Jewish child, the only one who ran around with other children, with the Jewish children.

Even though I was like one of them, things looked different to me than the other children in Sofiyovka. For example, when Christmas came around we'd have a Christmas tree, and we'd invite all the kids to our house to see it because they had no other opportunity to see a thing like that, to touch it, to smell it. It was a real attraction for a lot of them. To them, I was something different; but to me, they were the way normal children were.

——

Panas Mudrak

Panas was born in the village of Domashiv, close to Trochenbrod, in 1926 and lives there with his family today.

When I was eleven or twelve years old, I went to Sofiyovka with my father to sell and buy things. Then, during the war, after the killing, of course I had to go there because at least one man from each household had to work five days in that place, removing things from the buildings and dismantling the buildings, and I went with my father.

Before the war there was one street; they were paving the street. There were a lot of trades, a lot of shops, so people could buy anything. There was one very rich guy, Shwartz, who made leather for making boots, shoes, clothes.

I remember the post office, a factory that made dairy products like butter, and a factory that made leather. They would take their products to special markets on different days of the week for different kinds of products. Most people in Sofiyovka were buying and selling things—it was rare for someone to have fields and be working on the soil and making money from it—so they had to go to Olyka and the other places because it was their business.

In 1942, I remember when the Germans came, and they started killing the people near Yaromel. I was a small kid and it was far, and my parents were afraid for our lives. The Jews had to wear a special yellow circle on the front and back of their clothes so that they could be easily identified. People called them "Yud."

— —

VIRA SHULIAK

Vira was born in 1928. Her parents died when she was very young, and she was raised by her grandparents. Her grandfather was a forest ranger, and she spent her first years living in a house in the forest. Later they moved to Yosefin, and then, with a Ukrainian uncle married to a Polish woman, she moved to Przebradze, a Polish village. The Soviets changed the name of the village to Gayove, and Vira lives there still.

I was eleven when the war began. They killed the Jewish people first. The Germans destroyed Sofiyovka.

My grandparents used to take me to Sofiyovka because there were a lot of shops there where we could by a lot of things: different leather goods, even with fur.

The people who made those things, leather goods, the Germans let them live longer. First they killed those people who couldn't do such things that they valued, but in the end they were all killed anyway.

You could buy everything there: shoes, clothes, different products; there was even a restaurant there. So the people from all the villages around Sofiyovka went there to get everything they needed. You could get everything in Sofiyovka. Once the war started there was even more there because of the refugees. For example, there were watchmakers and dentists.

I remember two men from Trochenbrod: they stayed at our house. One was Chorni Moshko [Black Moshko], who was called that because he had a big black beard. Chorni Moshko sold bread; he would take a big sack of bread with him, and came to my village to sell them.

The second man who stayed at our house had red hair, he was sixteen or seventeen years old, and he had gotten a passport that said he was Polish or Ukrainian, not Jewish. So when people started to be killed he knew he had to run away, and he came to our house to say good-bye; we were crying because our family really loved him and were sorry he was leaving.

In Sofiyovka, most of the young men shaved, the older men had beards, like Chorni Moshko. One time I saw Chorni Moshko wrap a cloth around himself. I wanted to ask him what it was, but my mother said don't bother him, he's praying.

There were no differences among people—Jews, Poles, Ukrainians—in terms of dress. Before the war we lived in a very friendly way. There was no difference if you were Jewish, Polish, Ukrainian. But after the German occupation began something horrible started to happen. We heard first that they killed Jewish people near Yaromel; we heard their screaming, yelling, crying. It was horrible: here, in this place, we could hear their voices. And after that, in 1943, some kind of hatred started between Ukrainians and Polish, and they began killing each other. We organized a defense force here in Przebrodz; the other villages had this hatred so they sometimes burned each other's villages. It was the fault of the Germans; they made it important to kill each other.

——

Shmulik Potash

Shmulik Potash was born in Trochenbrod in 1920. He left in 1939 not long after the Soviets arrived in Trochenbrod, and over the next ten years made his way to what by then had become the State of Israel. Shmulik lives in Herzlia, a town just north of Tel Aviv, Israel.

Often in the middle of the night I think about Trochenbrod. I remember each house, one after the other. Every building, what it was, who was the head of the household, what kind of character he was, how many people lived in the house, who were the kids, and so on.

My mother was a good woman. Managing a household with lots of land, a big vegetable garden—tomatoes, potatoes, everything—four or five milk cows and a few more, and horses, chickens, and turkeys; cooking, washing clothes, cleaning, sewing, everything—where did she get the energy? On Fridays she'd get up at three in the morning to bake bread for the week for seven people! At the end of *Shabbat* she'd churn butter for the whole week. Not only that, she was a member of a social group that helped other people. To this day I don't understand how it's possible.

Life was hard in Trochenbrod. But with all the difficulties of life, I miss it. Of course you can't compare it to modern life, but there was a specialness about it, a good feeling, a feeling of community that I miss. We young people danced together, we sang together, we heard lectures and argued together about ideology, and there was a sense of fulfillment and satisfaction from that that kids today can't begin to know—what, are they going to get a feeling of satisfaction from hanging out at the mall?

— —

Szoel Rojtenberg

Szoel was born in Trochenbrod in 1922 and left with his family when he was eight years old. They went first to Portugal, where they had relatives, and then to Brazil, where he lives today in São Paulo. His family was very poor, and because of that, Szoel says he doesn't have happy childhood memories of Trochenbrod.

My father was the Cazone Rebbe, the Chief Rabbi appointed by the government, by Marshal Yuzef Pilsudski, to keep the official records of births, deaths, and so on. People were supposed to pay for his services, but usually they didn't. So there was very little money to support my father and his wife and eight children.

We had a big piece of land on the other side of the street in front of our house, and we would rent it out to other people to graze their cattle on. Behind our house we had a big garden with potatoes, and carrots, and apples, and pears, and lots of things.

I knew the whole Trochenbrod street, and never left Trochenbrod.

There were several butchers, but one slaughterhouse. The father of one of my friends had a building materials shop, where people could buy things for repairing their houses or building additions.

It was very cold in the winter; we'd have to bundle up, dress very warmly. Sometimes we'd sleep behind the stove to stay warm. We used to make improvised ice skates. We'd attach a wire underneath a small board, and we'd tie the board to our shoes, and we'd "skate" on the ice in the street in the winter. A group of us boys would do this together.

I remember a man who used to come from outside Trochenbrod with a horse-drawn fruit cart. A Gentile. The fruit on his cart was covered with a cloth, but he'd leave some fruits uncovered so customers could see what was for sale. Me and my group of friends would surround the cart and try to steal fruit. The fruitman would chase us away; sometimes he'd use his horsewhip. Once he hit me on my shoulder and back with the whip. My big brother came around and he was infuriated that the fruitman would whip me, so he overturned the fruit cart. And then the policeman (a Gentile) arrived. My brother had a little dog, who then started barking at the policeman. The policeman was very upset; he took out his gun and started shooting at the dog. My brother stuck out his hand to protect his dog, and got shot in the hand. There was no hospital; the policeman just wrapped his hand in white cloth.

Someone convinced my father, as the Cazone Rebbe, to change the age of a young woman from sixteen to eighteen, so she'd be the legal age to marry, and could marry her man. He was caught—the father of the bride denounced him—so his license was suspended and he was going to go to jail. So he left town with me and my mother, and we eventually came here to Brazil, and that's why I'm alive and wasn't killed like those who stayed.

––

EVGENIA SHVARDOVSKAYA

Evgenia was born in Trochenbrod in 1925 and was sixteen years old when she fled into the forest with her family to escape the murders. Her story of survival in the forest is similar to that of Basia-Ruchel Potash's family. Evgenia's family also was eventually found by partisans, and she fell in love with one, married him, and as a result has continued living in Lutsk, where she lives today. Evgenia is Basia-Ruchel's cousin.

I was in the *Beitar* organization, a Zionist organization. Many activities were done through *Beitar*, including plays and music. Life was good, with family and friends all around.

In the front portion of our house was another family that made the *matzos* for the whole town on *Pesach*. There was a special room attached to our house that was for *Sukkot*. We'd build a roof over it of branches, and you could see the stars through it.

Relations among Jews, Polish, and Ukrainians were good. The Polish people were customers in Trochenbrod shops. Ukrainians from the surrounding villages would shop there also.

When the Germans came they started killing from the first day. They began doing bad things to us because we had no right to live. They marked the houses with Jewish stars. We had no right to walk on the street. We hid. They took everything from us, especially any valuables.

They dug pits near Yaromel. Then they told everyone to take food for three days, leave their houses, and go with them. People took everything they could in the trucks with them. At the pits they killed everyone.

My father and his brother were expecting what

happened, so they had built false walls in sheds behind their houses for us to hide in. At night we all ran to the forest. We came back to the house of a Polish friend of my father, Vasily, in a nearby village, who let us stay for the night. But he told us that we had to leave because he couldn't risk being killed, since he had two sons.

We hid for a year and a half in the forest. At night some people, like Vasily, would bring some food. Sometimes people would let us take food from their fields. In spring 1944, the partisans found us and we stayed with them, and they took care of us. We cooked for them, cleaned their clothes. We were good friends with those partisans. They're all dead now. Alexander Felyuk died recently. Some of the partisans we were with were from Klubochin. Some were Jews, like Chaim Votchin and Gad Rosenblatt, who moved to Israel.

— —

THREE UKRAINIAN WOMEN

In June 2008, I stumbled across three colorfully dressed elderly women sitting on a bench in front of a house on a side lane in the village of Horodiche. Horodiche is four miles away from Trochenbrod southeast through the Radziwill forest. The women gave only their first names and patronymics, not their surnames: Sofia Panasivna, Ljubov Ivanivna, and Ustyma Denysivna. They became very animated when I began asking questions about Trochenbrod. They spoke as a group, with one completing or affirming the sentence of the other, taking turns commenting on any topic, and talking rapidly over and around each other—they obviously were very old friends. Here's a summary of what they said.

Sofiyovka people would come here to Horodiche to buy animals for the hides for their leather work. Sometimes they'd come here to sell fabric to make clothes, and other things. One Sofiyovka guy had a store here in Horodiche; Hershko was his name. They would bring . . . *matzah!*—that's what they called it!—that they baked for one of their holidays to share with us; it was good. I always waited for it.

On Saturday—they called it *Shabbos*—they wouldn't do any work. So someone else had to milk their cows for them on *Shabbos*.

My grandparents used to take me to Sofiyovka to go to the bathhouse.

I remember they had nice clothing stores there. But they had all kinds of stores, everything you could want. It was really a very nice place. The stores were mixed in with the houses. We were taken there often.

We all got along well with each other; we went to each other's villages. If Sofiyovka had survived, it would be bigger than Lutsk today. It was really fun there. They were good people, friendly people.

— —

Hanna Tziporen

Hanna was born in Trochenbrod in 1921. In 1939, at age eighteen, she left for Palestine by way of Vilna and the "Internat" way station there. She arrived in Palestine in 1941. Hana lives in Givatayim, a town just east of Tel Aviv, Israel.

Some people got out into the larger world, but ordinary people like me, when I started school at the age of seven, for us Trochenbrod was the whole world. There was a forest all around; there weren't dolls or many games for children, but there was always something to do, places to play.

When we were older, ten or twelve, we'd join a Zionist group. I joined *Beitar*. There we'd have programs, meetings, lectures—lectures mostly about *Eretz Yisrael*, its geography, the aspiring to it. Anshel Shpielman and Tuvia Drori were leaders.

During the week we were in public school. But our parents wanted us to know Hebrew, Yiddish, how to write a letter in Yiddish. For that we had private teachers. On *Shabbat* we'd get together. In the summer it was really nice, we'd get together in the forest. We'd have discussions with our leaders, and we'd practice drilling . . . left, right, left, right. We were training ourselves to be soldiers for *Eretz Yisrael*.

In our town there was a *Talmud Torah*, and many boys would study there. And after that, many boys would go to study in a yeshiva, away from the town, in one of the cities. The girls would often go to one of the nearby cities—Lutsk, Rovno—to learn a trade. I went to Lutsk.

My father supplied flour. On Sunday evening he'd go to the flour mill that there was in our town, and he'd fill up his cart with sacks of flour. Large families would buy a bag of flour, and stores also would buy them. My father also made the *matzot* for *Pesach*. They used to prepare the *matzot* by hand. Then my father brought a machine, and they'd begin to bake the *matzot* immediately after *Purim*, and up until *Pesach*. My father had a special wood-burning oven for that. It would cut up the dough into the pieces. I remember that the children were so fascinated by it.

There were craftsmen who would go out from Trochenbrod to the villages and had all sorts of businesses. They would sleep there if they had a job there, and come back on Friday. For example, there was one who went around to villages in the area and collected hair that could be used for brush bristles. He would bring it to someone in Trochenbrod that would prepare it for bristle-making and then sell it to businesses in Lutsk and Rovno that made brushes.

And we had dairies. Many families had one or two cows. They would milk them, and take the milk to the dairy, and the dairy would make cheese, cream, and even butter. They would sell these products in Lutsk, and even in Rovno. And there were tanneries and leather working. They sold the leather and they made shoes and boots. We also had carpenters. They would work in the surrounding villages, or people would come to the workshops in Trochenbrod and order furniture. There were house builders, and roofers who worked in both wood shakes [shingles] and thatch. There were two or three oil presses; people would bring the seeds from the surrounding villages to be pressed. Oil was also sold in the grocery stores, and people would come from the surrounding villages to buy it.

They were dressed nicely; the men in Western-style suits. No one dressed like Hasidim.[2] My father, for example, would go to the synagogue dressed in a suit, like in the city. Whether they were religious or not, everyone went to *shul* and observed the Jewish holidays. There were a few Communists, and they would go out on Friday night with their cigarettes, and people would pass them and taunt them yelling, "fire, fire."

We had nothing in common with Poles and Ukrainians. The opposite: they would come and do business, buy and sell . . . I remember that my father's grandmother would go out to villages with her husband, and she would bring all sorts of goods to sell, eggs and so on, and later the villagers would come to our house to buy things. There was no sense of hatred, but sometimes . . . the Gentiles, on Sundays, would walk through Trochenbrod on the way to their church. And sometimes, I remember once in particular, they did a little pogrom on us; maybe we were

2. Plural of Hasid, Hasidic Jews.

at fault also. As children maybe we shouted at them or put something in their way in the street. We weren't friends, but we got along.

We would prepare for winter. People who had root cellars would gather the potatoes, for example, and store them there. Those who didn't have root cellars would dig a pit in the ground, and put in the potatoes, and cover it with lots and lots of straw and soil. Because as *Pesach* would approach, people needed lots of potatoes, and potatoes didn't grow in the winter. It didn't always work. Sometimes the cold made it so that it was impossible to use them. There was always a great effort to prepare all kinds of foods that would last throughout the winter.

It's really sad that there's nothing left of Trochenbrod. I left Trochenbrod in 1939. I would never have believed, until I saw it myself, that there's nothing left. It hurts a great deal. In Trochenbrod—it's not just that I grew up there—in Trochenbrod there grew up a wonderful youth, wonderful people. It was a generation of people . . . there was joy, not bitterness; I think the political youth movements created it; it gave us a sense of purpose and meaning. Among the youth there was idealism. We were a Jewish town. That was unique. That was special.

GLOSSARY OF HEBREW AND YIDDISH TERMS

ebrew and Yiddish words often have a guttural "kh" sound in them, as in "khutzpah." In English transliterations, that sound is most often denoted with "ch." Unfortunately, "ch" is also pronounced as in "cheese." In the text I follow the most common practice and use "ch" for both sounds. If the "ch" should be pronounced as in "khutzpah" I denote that with a "(kh)" symbol in the table below: otherwise pronounce the "ch" as in cheese.

Balagola Wagon owner.

Baruch (kh) atoh adoinoi eiloiheinu melech (kh) haoilom . . . Opening phrase of many Hebrew blessings: "Blessed are you lord, our god, king of the universe . . ." The style of pronunciation that that Ryszard learned was the Ashkenazic, or European, style of Hebrew pronunciation.

Beitar Right-leaning Zionist youth organization that stressed self-defense.

Challah (kh) Egg bread, often braided, traditionally eaten by Jews on the Sabbath and holidays.

Chalutz, pl. chalutzim (kh) Pioneer; specifically, a Jewish settler in Palestine who went with the idea of paving the way for a Jewish state there.

Chapper (kh) Kidnapper of young Jewish teenagers for conscription into the Russian army in place of the sons of wealthy Jews.

Chazan (kh) Cantor.

Cheder (kh) Religious day-school for boys, usually held in the home of its only teacher.

Chulunt Slow-cooked stew that was a Sabbath specialty because it could be placed on the stove before the Sabbath and left there over a very low fire for the entire Sabbath, during which lighting a fire is forbidden.

Dreidel Spinning top, a toy traditionally used for Hanukah games.

Eretz Yisrael The Land of Israel; refers to the biblical Land of Israel and the Jewish homeland.

Etzel National Military Organization, a militant Jewish organization in Palestine that believed in creating a Jewish state there by using force against the British and Arabs.

Feltcher Self-taught paramedic, a healer, often also the pharmacy owner.

Goy Gentile.

Hanukah, or Chanukah (kh) Festival of Lights, an eight-day festival commemorating the reopening of the Hebrew Temple in Jerusalem in the second century B.C.E., following the military victory of Judah Maccabee. The holiday occurs in the same season as Christmas.

Hanukah gelt Coins given to children during the Hanukah holiday.

Kapoteh Long black or white kaftan, prayer garb.

Kichel Sweet cracker.

Kiddush Prayer sanctifying the Sabbath.

Latkes Potato pancakes, a traditional Hanukah dish.

Matzah, pl. matzot or matzos Unleavened flatbread eaten during Passover. In the plural, "matzot" represents the Sephardic, or Mediterranean style of Hebrew pronunciation that is used for modern Hebrew, and "matzos" represents the Ashkenazic, or European style of Hebrew pronunciation that was used in Europe for prayer, religious study, and other religious purposes.

Melamed Learned teacher.

Mitzvah A good deed in God's eyes.

Pesach (kh) Passover.

Purim The Festival of Lots, a happy holiday in the Jewish calendar that falls about a month before Passover.

Seder Passover ritual meal.

Shabbat, Shabbos Sabbath. "Shabbat" represents the Sephardic, or Mediterranean style of Hebrew pronunciation that is used for modern Hebrew, and "Shabbos" represents the Ashkenazic, or European style of Hebrew pronunciation that was used in Europe for prayer, religious study, and other religious purposes.

Shabbos goy "Sabbath Gentile" who performed functions for Jews like stoking fires or milking cows on the Sabbath because Jews are prohibited by religious law from performing acts of "work" on that day.

Shalom aleichem (kh) "Peace upon you," a traditional Jewish greeting.

Shoah Hebrew for "Holocaust."

Shtetl Community of Jews that was part of an Eastern European town. The Jews would live in a section that was exclusively Jewish and reflected Jewish religious traditions and values: in effect a Jewish village within a Gentile town. People referred to Trochenbrod also as a shtetl because the Yiddish word literally means "townlet."

Shul Synagogue. Derived from "school."

Sukkah Temporary field hut erected for the Feast of Tabernacles.

Sukkot, Sukkos Jewish fall harvest holiday, the Feast of Tabernacles, during which meals are taken in temporary huts where stars can be seen through fronds on the roof. "Sukkot" represents the Sephardic, or Mediterranean style of Hebrew pronunciation that is used for modern Hebrew, and "Sukkos" represents the Ashkenazic, or European style of Hebrew pronunciation that was used in Europe for prayer, religious study, and other religious purposes.

Talmud Torah Jewish day school for boys that has a number of teachers and teaches the classic Jewish religious texts.

Tzimmes Baked dish of mixed ingredients like chopped carrots, dried fruit, and meat.

Tzitzis Tassels on the corners of prayer shawls.

Yom Kippur Day of Atonement; the most important day on the Jewish calendar.

Zmires As used here, Sabbath songs.

CHRONOLOGY

1791   Czarina Catherine the Great establishes Russia's Jewish Pale of Settlement, an area that eventually extends from the Baltic Sea to the Black Sea.

1795   The last of three partitions of Poland leaves Poland's eastern lands, including Volyn province in which Trochenbrod will arise, in the hands of Russia's Catherine the Great and the czars who follow her.

1804   A decree of Czar Alexander I permits Jews to live only in larger towns and cities of the Pale of Settlement. The decree also exempts from harsh taxes and other discriminatory laws Jews who engage in agriculture on unused land. In the years following this decree the first individual Jewish families settle in the marshy Trochim Ford clearing.

1813   The first baby is born in Trochenbrod.

1820   An organized group of Jewish families from cities in the surrounding area joins the earlier Trochenbrod settlers.

1827   Czar Nicholas I issues a decree that conscripts Jewish boys into the Russian army until age forty-five. Again, families of Jewish farmers on unused land are exempted. In response, there is a new surge of Jewish settlement at Trochenbrod and outright purchase of the land by the settlers.

The United States is just over fifty years old.

1828   Approximately at this time a group of twenty-one families of Mennonites establishes the villages of Yosefin and Sofiyovka near Trochenbrod. They begin to abandon these settlements several years later.

1835   Another decree from Czar Nicholas I requires rural Jews to be in agricultural "colonies" and have passports and permits to travel. Trochenbrod is formally recognized as a Jewish agricultural colony and given the name of the former Mennonite village, Sofiyovka.

1837   Ignatovka, also known as Lozisht, is established near Trochenbrod as a sister Jewish agricultural colony.

1850   A new decree outlaws Hasidic dress. From this point on Trochenbrod is gradually de-Hasidized, though it remains strongly religious.

1865   Another Czarist decree allows Jews to change their status from farm villager to town dweller without giving up their land. The Jews of Sofiyovka petition for and are granted town status; Ignatovka remains a colony.

America's Civil War ends.

Tolstoy begins publishing *War and Peace* in serial form.

1880   Trochenbrod begins a process of steady economic diversification, modernization, and growth, increasingly transforming itself into a real town and regional commercial center. This process continues until the First World War.

The first Trochenbrod immigrant goes to the United States.

1882   Czar Alexander III enacts the "May Laws," highly oppressive anti-Jewish regulations that restrict where Jews can live, how many can receive higher education, and the professions they are allowed to practice. These regulations remain in effect until the 1917 revolution, and are one factor encouraging massive Jewish emigration from Russia during that period.

1885   Heavy emigration from Sofiyovka begins and continues to 1940, except during the First World War. Trochenbroders immigrate to North and South America, and after the First World War also to Palestine.

1897   Trochenbrod and Lozisht have a population of close to sixteen hundred Jews. Trochenbrod begins to have light industry, begins to modernize, and begins to diversify into a larger array of economic activities.

The economy of the entire Pale of Settlement becomes more dependent on industrial production.

1901   Theodore Roosevelt becomes president of the United States.

1904   The Russo-Japanese war spurs illicit emigration of many Trochenbrod men to avoid conscription.

1914   The First World War places Trochenbrod on the front between Austro-Hungarian and Russian troops, where it suffers pillage, rape, murder, famine, forced labor, and disease.

1917   The October Revolution establishes Soviet rule in Russian lands.

1918   The First World War ends; the newly constituted Soviet Union immediately embarks on a territorial struggle with Poland. Trochenbrod is further ravaged in the conflict.

1921   Trochenbrod is now located in eastern Poland. Its population is again roughly sixteen hundred Jews.

1925   Prince Radziwill begins building a Catholic church at the edge of Trochenbrod to serve Polish people living in villages in the area.

Trochenbrod begins to recover and reassert itself with vigor as a regional commercial center.

1929   Sófiyovka is described in the *Illustrated Directory of Volhyn* and the *Polish Address Business Directory* in a way that suggests it has begun to reclaim its role as a robust regional commercial center.

1933   In this year and the next, many Trochenbroders who

had settled in the United States return to visit their relatives in Trochenbrod.

1934   Hitler, as both chancellor and *Führer* in Germany, emerges as a major political figure in Europe.

A Polish-German nonaggression pact allows for unrestricted Nazi propaganda in Poland. From 1934 on, Poland's pogroms and repression of Jews are lesser echoes of those in Germany.

1938   The first military training course for *Etzel* officers is conducted in Trochenbrod.

November 10: Kristallnacht.

1939   Spring: A ribbon-cutting ceremony is conducted for the first paved segment of Trochenbrod's street. Trochenbrod has some electricity, telegraph and telephone, newspapers from Warsaw, bicycles, movies, and even an occasional visit by a motorized vehicle; the town is rapidly expanding and modernizing.

August: Germany and the U.S.S.R. sign the Molotov-Ribbentrop Nonaggression Pact.

September: Germany and the U.S.S.R. invade and divide Poland between them. The Second World War begins. Trochenbrod comes under Soviet rule.

1941   The population of Trochenbrod and Lozisht has swelled to over six thousand people as a result of economic growth in the interwar years and an influx of refugees from western Poland in the wake of the German invasion.

June 22: Germany invades and the Soviets withdraw

from eastern Poland, leaving Trochenbrod in Nazi hands. Trochenbrod is terrorized and brutalized by the Germans and their Ukrainian auxiliary police. December: Pearl Harbor is attacked; America enters the Second World War.

1942   August 11: The first *Aktion*. Most of the Jews of Trochenbrod and Lozisht are taken to pits prepared near Yaromel and slaughtered.

September 21: The second *Aktion*. On *Yom Kippur*, everyone remaining in Trochenbrod's ghetto, including many that had fled from the first *Aktion* and then returned to pray with their brothers on *Yom Kippur*, is taken to the Yaromel pits and murdered.

December: The third *Aktion*. The last of Trochenbrod's people, about twenty leather workers, are shot.

1950   A Trochenbrod survivor living in the nearby city of Lutsk reports having visited the site of the town and finding no remaining physical evidence of it.

SOURCES

A Grandfather's Memories. Memoir of Morris Wolfson, as told to his grandaughter, Geri Wolfson Fuhrmann, in November, 1974; submitted by Geri Wolfson Fuhrmann as a term paper to Sol Gittleman, Professor of Yiddish Literature, Tufts University, in December, 1974. The manuscript was given to me in 2008 by Laura Praglin, cousin of Geri Wolfson Fuhrmann; Laura and Geri subsequently provided a tape and CD of the full interview and related material. Morris (Moshe) Wolfson was the son of Wolf Schuster, a shoemaker in Trochenbrod. Wolf immigrated to the United States, and in 1912 brought over his son Moshe. When during immigration processing Moshe was asked his father's name in order to establish the surname, Moshe said he was Wolf's son: duly recorded as Wolfson, and that remained Moshe's legal family name forever after.

A Voice from the Forest: Memoirs of a Jewish Partisan. By Nahum Kohn and Howard Roiter; published by Holocaust Library, New York, 1980. Like many Polish Jews, after the Nazis arrived Nahum Kohn fled eastward, to what a short time before had been eastern Poland. He eventually found his way to Trochenbrod. After a few months he left Trochenbrod for the forest and established a Jewish partisan unit that included young men from Trochenbrod. He operated in the region around Trochenbrod for the duration of the war, and afterward settled in Canada.

And I Still See Their Faces: Images of Polish Jews. Published by the American-Polish-Israeli Shalom Foundation, located in Warsaw, Poland, 1997. In 1994, the Shalom Foundation appealed throughout Poland for photographs of Jewish friends and neighbors before the Holocaust. More than seven thousand photos came in, accompanied by notes telling what the submitters knew about the people in them. A jury selected photos, editors refined the notes, and the result is this beautiful and moving book. As I explain in the Epilogue, *And I Still See Their Faces* ultimately brought Basia-Ruchel Potash and Ryszard Lubinski back together; this in turn led me to most of the photographs of Trochenbrod in the 1930s that appear in this book.

Ani Ma'amin: Eidut V'Hagot (I Believe: Testimony and Meditations). By Tuvia Drori; published in Hebrew by Yair Publications, Tel Aviv, Israel, 1994. The author gave me an original edition of this book in 1997. Joseph Blau translated the manuscript to English, and a copy of that translation was given to me in 1998 by Marvin Perlman, a Trochenbrod descendant living in Potomac, Maryland. I have edited the English translation of quotations that appear in this book. It was in *Ani Ma'amin* that I found a reference to Jacob Banai's book, "Anonymous Soldiers" (Hebrew, Friends Publishing, Tel Aviv, 1978) in which he records his impressions of Trochenbrod while on the 1938 *Etzel* officers training course.

Esh Achazah B'ya'ar (*A Forest Ablaze*). By Gad Rosenblatt; published by HaKibbutz HaMeuchad Publishing House, Ltd., Kibbutz Lochamei Haghettaot, Israel, first published in 1957, corrected second edition published in 1976. In 2008, Burt and Ellen Singerman provided me with an informal translation into English.

Findings of the [Soviet] Commission Documenting Fascist Atrocities. Report of a local commission set up by Soviet authorities, February 1945. This report, which is based on witness testimony, describes Holocaust events in the Sofiyovka area and provides some interesting insights into the Soviet view of what transpired. The report, housed in the State Archive of Volyn Region in Lutsk, Ukraine, was translated for me by Alexander Dunai of Lviv, Ukraine.

Hailan V'shoreshav (*The Tree and Its Roots: The History of T.L., Sofiyovka-Ignatovka*). Edited by Y. Vainer, T. Drori,

G. Rosenblatt, A. Shpielman; published primarily in Hebrew and Yiddish by Bet TAL, Givatayim, Israel, 1988. Bet TAL is the organization of people from Trochenbrod and the neighboring village of Lozisht and people descended from them; *Hailan* is the "official" memorial book for Trochenbrod: it can be viewed on the Bet Tal Web site, http://bet-tal.com.

The Holocaust by Bullets: A Priest's Journey to Uncover the Truth Behind the Murder of 1.5 Million Jews. By Father Patrick Desbois; Published by Palgrave Macmillan, New York, 2008. In this book, Father Desbois describes his mission to document the murder of the Jews of Ukraine, particularly western and southern Ukraine, by German killing units (*Einzatsgruppen*). Some of the details of his findings helped me sort through disparate reports of what actually happened in Trochenbrod and arrive at the probable facts of that case. Father Desbois's organization is Yahad-In Unum, www.yahadinunum.org.

Ilustrowany Przewodnik po Wolyniu (*Illustrated Directory of Volyn*), *1929*. I have an excerpt of pages from this document—including a photo of a Volyn landscape—that describes Sofiyovka, Kivertzy, Rozische, and other towns in the Trochenbrod area. I have no record of how this came into my hands.

Księga adresowa Polski (*Polish Address Directory, 1929*. By W. M. Gdanskiem; published by Towarzystwo Reklamy Miedzynarodowe, Warsaw, Poland. A portion of this directory, containing businesses by town in Volyn Province, including Sofiyovka, was first provided to me in 1999 by Dr. Yale J. Reisner, who was working for the Ronald S. Lauder Foundation in Warsaw, Poland.

Mennonite Historical Atlas, Second Edition. Text and some maps by Helmut T. Huebert, and maps by William Schroeder; published by Springfield Publishers, Winnipeg, Canada, 1996. An excerpt from the Atlas dealing with Volyn, together with several maps, was sent to me in 1998 by Helmut T. Huebert.

My Townlet–Trachenbrod: A Chain of Memories. By David Shwartz; published in Yiddish and English by Elisha Press, Tel Aviv, Israel, 1954. David Shwartz was born in Trochenbrod in 1880. He was already married to his wife Miriam when he left Trochenbrod alone in 1907 and began earning money in Columbus, Ohio. He returned to Trochenbrod and brought his wife and children back to Columbus just before World War I broke out. He visited Trochenbrod again, with his wife, in 1934. He wrote his memoir in 1939, but only printed it as a booklet fifteen years later. David died in 1960, Miriam eight years after him. David and Miriam Shwartz left behind what is today a large family of grandchildren, great-grandchildren, and other relatives.

Pinkas Hekehilot (Encyclopedia of Jewish Communities from their Founding until Just after the Holocaust and Second World War),

Volume 5, Volyn and Polesia. By Shmuel Spektor; published in Hebrew by Yad Vashem, The Holocaust Martyrs and Heroes Remembrance Authority, 1990, Jerusalem, Israel. I was guided to this volume and additional materials in 2009 by Michlean Amir, reference archivist at the United States Holocaust Memorial Museum.

Russia to New York. By Jeanne Glass Kokol. Jeanne Kokol was born in Trochenbrod in 1913 as Shaindeleh Ruchel Gluz. She came to the United States in 1921. She wrote this memoir for her family in about 2002, and died in Florida in 2007. Thomas C. Spear gave me this memoir in 2008, after obtaining it from Irving Kokol, Jeanne's son. Thomas's and Irving's great-great-grandfathers were brothers.

Shmilike Drossner's Trachenbrod. An oral history by Shmilike Drossner, primarily but not only about how Jewish holidays were observed in Trochenbrod before World War I; told to and transcribed by Samuel Sokolow in the 1970s. In 2008, Burt and Ellen Singerman and Robbie Ross Tisch separately gave me copies of this oral history.

Sofievka (Trochenbrod). An article originally written in Hebrew and submitted to the Yad Vashem (Shoah memorial) archives in Jerusalem by Gad Rosenblatt (see *Esh Achazah BaYa'ar—A Forest Ablaze*, above). Marvin Perlman (see *Ani Maamin: Eidut V'Hagot—I Believe: Testimony and Meditations*, above) gave me an English translation of the article in 1998.

Trochenbrod (*Sofiyevka*). An article by Eliezer Barkai (Burak) published in Hebrew in the journal *Yalkut Volyn*, ("Anthology of Volyn") Issue #1; published by Archion Volyn B'Eretz-Yisrael (Volyn Archives in Palestine) and Irgun Yotzei Volyn B'Eretz Yisrael (Organization of Emigrés from Volyn in Palestine), Tel Aviv, April 1945. This article can be read in Hebrew or English on the Bet TAL Web site, http://bet-tal.com. The article was first brought to my attention in 1999 by Dr. Yale J. Reisner, working for the Ronald S. Lauder Foundation in Warsaw.

Trochenbrod: The Life and Death of a Shtetl in the Ukraine. By Morton L. Kessler; a thesis paper submitted for an M.A. degree to the Graduate School of John Carroll University, Cleveland, 1972. Morton Kessler was the son of an immigrant from Trochenbrod; his paper was based in part on a large number of interviews with immigrants from Trochenbrod living in the United States.

Other sources that I drew upon for this book include:

- Photographs of Trochenbrod and Trochenbroders that I obtained from Laura Beeler, Marlene Berman, Marilyn Weiner Bernhardt, Miriam Antwarg Ciocler, Betty Potash Gold, Phyllis Grossman, Alyn Levin-Hadar, Ryszard Lubinski, Burt and Ellen Singerman, Anne Weiner, and *Hailan V'Shoreshav* (cited above);
- The Antwarg, Blitzstein, Burak, Foer, Gilden, Gluz,

Gotman, Kerman, Kimelblat, Pearlmutter, Potash, Roitenberg, Schuster, Sheinbein, Szames, and Zucker families,
who provided me with firsthand Trochenbrod stories or
stories handed down from their forebears;

- Film footage of twenty interviews with people born in
Trochenbrod or living in nearby villages, shot in Israel,
the United States, and Ukraine by Itai Tamir and a
Transfax Film Productions crew (www.transfax.co.il) for
the Israeli Bet TAL organization (http://bet-tal.com),
which graciously made the footage available to me;

- Videotapes of elderly individuals reminiscing about their
lives in Trochenbrod, which were given to me by their
respective descendants;

- Maps—Austro-Hungarian, German, Polish, Russian,
Soviet, Ukrainian and U.S. military—spanning the period
1706–2006;

- Videotape of four trips to the site of Trochenbrod by
groups primarily of Israelis, including the visit in 1992
of Israelis and two Americans to erect the black marble
monuments at Trochenbrod and at the mass grave
site;

- Interviews with people born in Trochenbrod who now live
in Israel, Brazil, North America, Poland, and Ukraine;

- Interviews with a number of Ukrainians living in the Trochenbrod area who remember Trochenbrod from their
childhood or youth;

- Conversations with Ukrainians who now live or used to
live in villages near the site of Trochenbrod;

- My own photographs and video footage of the site of Trochenbrod and the surrounding area;
- Explorations of the Trochenbrod terrain by foot and tractor with my friend Ivan Podziubanchuk and his family from the nearby village of Domashiv, during my nine visits to the area in the period 1997–2009.

ACKNOWLEDGMENTS

I want first to thank Jessica Case, my editor at Pegasus Books. Jessica happily took me and my manuscript under her wing and devoted untold hours skillfully helping refine the manuscript and bringing the book to the widest possible English readership. She has been a wonderful partner from whom I've learned a great deal, and has been a pleasure to work with.

Another person who has been instrumental in helping me bring the story of Trochenbrod to life is my literary agent, Jonah Straus. Jonah immediately understood what this book was and could be, was enthusiastic about it, and worked hard to find the right publisher and an international readership. He, too, has been a pleasure to work with.

I want also to thank Michael Millman, Senior Editor, Praeger Publishing, and all the others at Praeger who considered and encouraged this book.

It's amazing—and wonderful—how many people gave of themselves for this project. It's only because they gladly shared so much so freely that I was able to put this book together, and help Trochenbrod live on beyond our lifetimes. I can't thank them enough.

In Israel there was:
Michal Barry, who helped with Hebrew-to-English translation during interviews with Shmulik Potash;
Chaim and Mira Binnenbaum, who helped coordinate with Israeli interview subjects;
Joseph Blau, who helped with research and Hebrew-to-English translation;
Yehuda and Uri Dotan, who provided key video and photographic material;
Tuvia Drori, who shared his Trochenbrod stories over the course of many years;
Moshe Goler, who provided information about the Argentine Trochenbrod-Lozisht community;
Sarit Harpaz, who helped coordinate with Israeli interview subjects;
Henia Katzir, who shared her family's Trochenbrod stories and photos and provided information on the early days of the Israeli Trochenbrod-Lozisht community

and the postwar activities of her father, Eliezer (Burak) Barkai;

Moti Litvak, who helped coordinate with Israeli interview subjects;

Shmuel Potash, who shared his stories of Trochenbrod and his journey from Poland to Israel;

Noam Rosenblatt, who provided translation and liaison help concerning Gad Rosenblatt's partisan years;

Nachman Rotenberg, who shared his Trochenbrod stories, knowledge, and photos;

Itai Tamir, of Transfax Film Productions, who shot and made available important footage from Israel, Ukraine, and the United States;

Hana Tziporen, who shared her stories and photos of Trochenbrod and her journey from Poland to Israel; and

Chaim Votchin, who shared stories of his partisan years.

In North and South America there was:

Sol Ackman, who provided documents and information about the Baltimore–Washington, D.C., Trochenbrod community;

Michlean Amir, reference archivist at the United States Holocaust Memorial Museum, who offered valuable research guidance;

Laura Beeler, who provided Trochenbrod-related family photos;

Alexandra Belenkaya, who helped with Polish-to-English translation;

Marvin Bendavid, my brother, who accompanied me on my
first trip to the site of Trochenbrod and has supported
my research efforts ever since;

Naftali Bendavid, who helped with filming, interviewing,
critiquing, and editorial advice;

Leah Bendavid-Val, who helped with photographing, interviewing, and critiquing, and who traveled with me in
Ukraine. Leah also made major editorial contributions
and has been a very supportive partner in this project
and in the rest of my life;

Oren Bendavid-Val, who helped with filming, interviewing,
critiquing, and advising, and who also traveled with me
in Ukraine and Belarus;

Marlene Berman, who provided Trochenbrod-related family
photos;

Doreen Berne, who provided information about David
Shwartz and permission to incorporate his words;

Charles and Marilyn Bernhardt, who provided Trochenbrod-
related family photos;

Miriam Antwarg Ciocler, who shared Trochenbrod-related
family artifacts, photos, and photos of Trochenbrod
artifacts;

Anne Weiner Cohen, who provided photos and information
about the Baltimore–Washington, D.C., Trochenbrod
organization;

Father Patrick Desbois, who, with authority and a depth
of detail unavailable from any other source, explained
how the *Einzatsgruppen* operated. (I talked with Father

Desbois in the United States, but his headquarters are in Paris—see http://yahadinunum.org.)

Rose Blitzstein Elbaum, who provided an electronic version of the David Shwartz memoir;

Esther Safran Foer, who shared family stories and photos of Trochenbrod and the war years there, and who introduced me to Father Desbois;

Geri Wolfson Fuhrmann, who provided family print and oral Trochenbrod histories;

Mary Lou Garbin, who provided maps and research guidance on the Mennonites in the Trochenbrod area;

Betty Gold (Basia-Ruchel Potash), who shared her memories of Trochenbrod and the war period with me in great detail over an eleven-year period, and who helped to communicate with Ryszard Lubinski;

Jeremy Goldscheider, who was a partner in many filming and interviewing efforts;

Ronald Goldfarb, who encouraged my pursuit of publication of this book;

Phyllis Grossman, who provided Trochenbrod-related family photos;

Dr. Toby Helfand, who helped with Yiddish-to-English translation;

Betty Hellman (Peshia Gotman), who shared her memories of Trochenbrod;

Helmut T. Huebert, who provided research guidance and assistance, maps, and excerpts from the Mennonite Historical Atlas;

Ivan Katchanovski, who provided insights into events in the
Trochenbrod area during World War II and help with
Russian terms;

Chaim Kimelblat, who provided information about Jewish
resettlement in South America;

Merrill Leffler, who gave invaluable advice and guidance for
improving the manuscript for this book;

Alyn Levin-Hadar, who shared Trochenbrod family history
and photos;

Andrea Liss, who facilitated communication with her grandmother, Ida Liss, a native of Trochenbrod;

Ida Gilden Liss, who shared her memories of growing up in
Trochenbrod;

George L. Maser, whose prewar map of the Trochenbrod
region helped spur me to further research;

Israel Milner, who provided information about the Philadelphia Trochenbrod-Lozisht organization;

Laura Praglin, who provided family print and oral Trochenbrod histories;

Szoel Rojtenberg, who shared his memories of Trochenbrod;

Burt and Ellen Singerman, who provided Trochenbrod-
related family photos;

Olya Smolyanova, who helped with Russian-to-English and
Ukrainian-to-English translation;

Gary Sokolow, who shared Trochenbrod-related photographic and print material;

Sam Steinberg, who helped with Yiddish-to-English
translation;

Anne Weiner, who provided Trochenbrod-related family photos;

Olga Zachary, who helped with Ukrainian-to-English translation;

Agnieszka Zieminska, who helped with Polish-to-English translation; and

Eliana Zuckermann, who hosted me and coordinated interviews in Rio de Janeiro.

In Ukraine, Russia, and Poland there was:

Mikhailo Demchuk, who shared his memories of Trochenbrod and the war years;

Ustyma Denysivna, Ljubov Ivanivna, and Sofia Panasivna, who as a group in Horodiche shared their memories of Trochenbrod;

Alexander Dunai, who for ten years was my devoted driver, translator, researcher, guide, friend, and fellow adventurer in Ukraine—I could not have managed without him in that period;

Anatoliy Hrytsiuk, head of the Volyn Regional Council, and staff for their hospitality and their administrative and logistical support during field activities;

Ivan Kovalchuk, who shared his memories of Trochenbrod and the war years;

Anna, Eva, and Ivan Kurnyev, warm and generous Lutsk friends, who helped with field research, photography, research facilitation, and local communication in Ukraine;

Ryszard Lubinski, who with great generosity, openness, and warmth shared his memories and photos of Trochenbrod during lengthy interview sessions in Radom, Poland;

Panas Mudrak, who shared his memories of Trochenbrod and the war years;

Loiko Mykytivna (Eva Kurnyeva's mother), who shared her memories of Trochenbrod and the war years;

Vladislav Nakonieczny, who shared his memories and thoughts about Ukraine in the war years, the Communist era, and the early post-Communist era;

Vira Shuliak, who shared her memories of Trochenbrod and the war years;

Sergiy Omelchuk, a native of Lutsk, who helped with field research, photography, local communication, transportation, and logistical arrangements, who provided local representation for this project in the Lutsk-Trochenbrod area and has been a dear, reliable, and trusted friend since 2006;

Ivan and Nina Podziubanchuk, who together with their children Maria and Bogdan (most recently joined by new arrival Illya) have been taking me by tractor-wagon to the site of Trochenbrod, arranging interviews with old-timers in the villages of Domashiv and Yaromel, showing me villages and special places in the Trochenbrod region, connecting me with local officials, acquiring Trochenbrod artifacts and giving them to me as gifts, feeding me scrumptious rural Ukrainian meals topped off with homemade vodka, and generally being great friends for well over a decade;

Yale J. Reisner, who, from his position as Director of Research and Archives at the Ronald S. Lauder Foundation Genealogy Project at the Jewish Historical Institute of Poland, in Warsaw, generously provided me with my first Trochenbrod documents, documents that helped fire my imagination and interest;

Nikolai Romanov, who helped with Russian-to-English translation;

Meylakh Sheykhet, who in Lviv helped me understand Jewish prewar and wartime life in eastern Poland, now Ukraine, and the present-day complexities of trying to recapture elements of it;

Evgenia Shvardovskaya, who at the site of Trochenbrod, in Israel, and in Lutsk shared her memories of Trochenbrod; and

Yankel Szyc, who on my repeated visits to Poland served as my driver, guide, and translator.

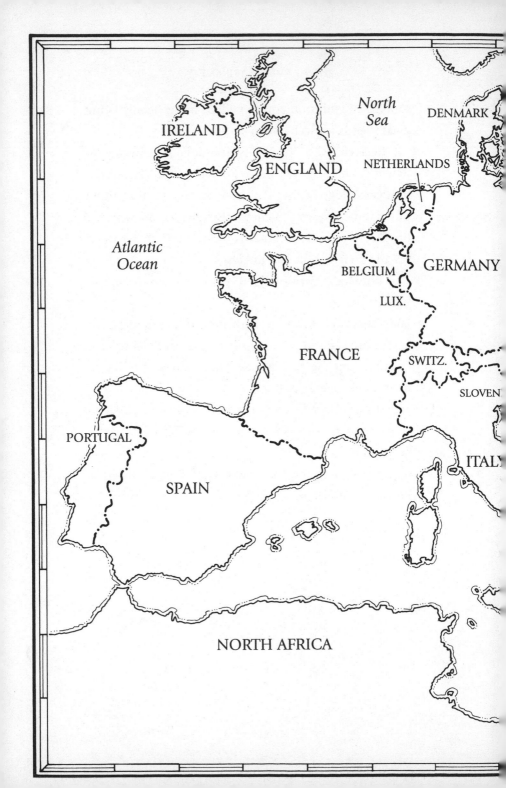